I Understand Beijing

I love Beijing

I ♥ Beijing

Wu Jisong

CHINA DEVELOPMENT PRESS

Welcome to Beijing

Beijing, a city with a long history, is the most potent symbol of Chinese culture. She is full of life and energy, radiant with the charm of modern civilization. As is known to all, Beijing has won the right to host the 2008 Summer Olympic Games. With such opportunity, Beijing and China, and indeed the whole world, have been offered a big moment for an epoch-making development.

Everyone from all over the world is welcomed here. We share one world, a world with peace and harmony. We have one dream, a dream expressing the aspiration of all peoples around the globe. We are in full confidence that our foreign friends will fall in love with Beijing after they come to know her. It is in here that you can experience the pulse of

history, feel the vitality of civilization and hear the melody of our shared dream.

Only after we become acquainted with each other can we become friends. Only after we get to know each other can we have more chances to cooperate. In his book *I Love Beijing,* Professor Wu Jisong draws on his 60 years of life experiences as a Beijing citizen, as well as his scholarly expertise, to open up to the reader a spectacular view of this colorful city. It is our belief that the book in your hands will not only increase your knowledge about Beijing, but will also strengthen your love for her.

Let us work together to fulfill our shared dream, hold hand in hand to create a beautiful tomorrow.

Mayor of Beijing , Executive President of Beijing
Organizing Committee for Games of the 29 Olympiad
Wang Qishan
March 22, 2007

王岐山
2007年3月22日

我爱北京

"I love Beijing". If you've experienced this great city, I have a feeling that is what you would like to say. We all come from the same world, and have a common dream.

I have traveled across China and around the world, I've circled the globe 30 times – a total distance of 1.2 million kilometers. I've left my footprints in all of China's 34 provinces, cities, municipalities and special administrative regions. I have been to 300 cities in 80 countries and regions. I've lived in Paris for 6 years, and in cities like Tokyo, Seoul, New York, Rio De Janeiro, Moscow, London, Berlin, Stockholm, Cairo, Sydney etc. for periods ranging from one week up to one year. In Asia, from Tokyo of Japan to Istanbul of Turkey, from Novosibirsk of Russia to Djakarta of Indonesia; In Europe, from Lisboa of Portugal to Perm of Russia, from Uppsala of Sweden to Catania of Italy; In America, from Vancouver of Canada to Santiago of Chile; In Africa, from Rabat of Morocco to Cape Town of South Africa, from Nairobi of Kenya to Lome in Togo; In Australia, from Sydney on the east coast to Perth in the west. I've been to all those places. Is your hometown on this list?

I am fond of those cities, as all of them have charming places, and friendly and easy-going people. But whenever I return to Beijing, I love it even more than before. Travel helps one realize what it means to love home, and comparison deepens this love. When you leave Beijing, I'm sure that you will love your hometown even more than before.

I have been living in Beijing for 60 years, and would like to take this opportunity to take you on a six-day tour of my hometown. Beijing is a lively international metropolis with a long history, beautiful scenery, rich culture, and a developed science and education system. Five hundred thousand years ago, the ape-like Peking Man was living here. Beijing has been a city for 3000 years. Early on, the walled city had an area of 4 hectares, and could be ranked as a medium-sized city in the world of that time. Beijing became a capital city in 938 A.D., 30 years earlier than Cairo of Egypt. To the north of Beijing sit the Yan Mountains. To the west, it has the West Mountains, covered with virgin forest. To the north runs the Wenyu River. To the south the famous Jing-Hang canal flows toward Hangzhou, and the Yongding River skirts the capital on the west. Lying at the boundary between the land of nomads and farmers, Beijing has been the capital of China 6 times. Its rich cultural heritage shows the influence of many different people groups. Nowdays, Beijing is home to China's best universities, its largest science park, 160 branches of Global 500 corporations as well as many branches of five out of the world's ten largest retailers. Beijing is the highway, railway and aviation centre of China, with the annual number of passengers at Beijing Capital Airport reaching up to 41 million. About 100 thousand foreigners live here. Beijing has really turned into an international modern metropolis.

Beijing is home to the largest palace kept intact in the world — the Forbidden City, representation of Chinese traditional architecture, whose area is four times that of the Louvre in Paris. Beijing has one of the largest imperial gardens in the world—the Summer Palace. Its construction area is one and a half times the area of Versailles. It's interesting to note that of the five main kinds of gardens found in the world, the city of Beijing has four. In the suburbs of Beijing can be found the emperor's mausoleum, in size second only to the Pyramid – the imperial mausoleum in the suburbs of Cairo. Many religions can be found in Beijing, such as Buddhism, Christianity, and Islam, as well as one of China's own religions, Taoism. The Peking Opera is the Chinese opera, the quintessence of China. Peking Quanjude roast duck is the best of Chinese cuisine, and handicrafts such as Beijing's Closionne enjoy a high reputation the world over.

Traditional housing in Beijing has its own characteristics. Siheyuan (Dwelling Compounds) and Hutongs are both unique in the world. Currently, the habitable space per person in Beijing is 20 square meters, with 11 square meters of "green land" per person. In Beijing, you can easily find restaurants offering French, Japanese, American, Russian, German, Italian, Korean and Brazilian food, and most of them can serve in English.

" New Beijing, New Olympics" is the slogan for the 2008 Olympic Games. Beijing will be the host city of the 2008 Olympics, which will contribute to the world's harmony. I had the privilege of participating in the Olympic bidding process. Following the concept of a " high-tech, people-friendly and environment-friendly Olympic Games", Beijing has been preparing for this big event. It has not only built and remodeled numbers of stadiums, but also made considerations for their post-Olympic use. Not only has Beijing increased "its green land" area , but it has also implemented The Capital City Sustainable Water Resources Program to guarantee its water supply. The purpose of this program is to improve the water system, and repair the ecosystem of Beijing. As a result, we have not only adopted many new forms of high technology, but also enhanced the awareness of Beijing's citizens to shoulder their responsibilities to protect the environment. Through the Olympic Games, we want to promote the personal culture of the general population, encouraging them to exert their creativity. We also want to implement a recycling economy, and boost thc sustainable development of the city. Thus the Beijing Olympics will be an "ecological, knowledge-based and sustainable Olympics".

Besides watching the Olympic Games, you will be a visitor of Beijing as well. Beijing is the vivid epitovne of China's past history and current developments. Its marvelous speed of growth often makes me, who have been living here for 60 years, unable to recognize some of the newly built or rebuilt areas. It is certain that you will love Beijing, as we come from the same world — our planet Earth. It is certain that you will love Beijing, for we have a common dream for peace and development. As you look back on the history of Beijing, you can see its struggle for justice and peace, and you can see sustainable development as you look forward into Beijing's future. After visiting Beijing, you will have a deeper impression of the diversity of our world, as well as a deeper understanding of our dreams.

As you come to my hometown, I am honored to take you on this six-day tour, and offer you this booklet. The journey you are about to embark on condenses 60 years of my feelings into 6 days. How many days will you be traveling in Beijing? Of course, it's up to you. I have been to 80 countries around the world, and I don't know whether I have been to your homeland, or met you yet, but being a world traveler, I will try to satisfy your needs in whatever way possible. If there is something missing in this book, please do not hesitate to write me, and I will try my best to answer your questions in the next edition.

吴季松

Wu Jisong

Feb.18. 2007

Contents

History of Beijing 1

Cultural Heritage in Beijing 16

Culture Heritages in the Suburbs of Beijing 40

Religion and Confucianism in Beijing 60

Education, Science & Technology and Environment 70

Foods and Business of Beijing 76

Folk Houses of Beijing 93

The Culture of Beijing 102

Appendix 111

Beijing lies in the north of China, at 39° north latitude and 116° east longitude, belonging to the temperate climate zone. The ecosystem here is characterized by arbor wood and shrubbery mixed with herbaceous plants. The administrative area of Beijing covers 16,400 square kilometers, with the population of 15.8 million. The planed area of the city is 1,070 square kilometers with the population of approximate 9 million. The old Beijing inner city is 57 square kilometers with the population of 1.2 million. The weather is a bit hot during late June and early August, and is fairly cold from late December through early February. The best season to tour Beijing is from late April to the middle of June, or from mid- August to early November.

History of Beijing

Beijing is a city with a long history. According to archaeological findings, the city has existed for more than 3,000 years. Beijing has been a capital city for more than 800 years.

1. Before being the capital

Half a million years ago The complete skull of Peking Man was discovered by archeologists and historians in 1927 in the 70-meters high Dragon Bone Hill of Zhoukoudian, Fangshan District, in the southwest suburbs of Beijing. And a total of more than 200 skull fragments belonging to over 40 individuals of different ages and sexes were uncovered along with many stone tools. This was the earliest ape-man found in Beijing. The site was listed by the United Nations' Educational, Scientific and Cultural Organization (UNESCO) as one of the world's heritages. Some stone tools of the same period were also discovered at the Wangfujing construction site in central Beijing.

The cave where Peking Man was discovered.

Is Peking Man from Africa as well?

Beijing's Huairou Jiankou Great Wall covered in a vast and boundless sea of clouds.

Remaining sections of the Great Wall in Beijing: the Mutianyu Great Wall.

Early Neolithic Age: Ten thousand years ago In East Hulin Village of Mentougou District in west Beijing, 25 kilometers from the city centre, a tomb containing three bodies dating back to the Neolithic age, was discovered in 1966. It is believed that at that time Beijing's weather was cool and humid, and landscape was mainly covered by needle leaf mix broadleaf forest and grassland.

Late Neolithic Age: Five thousand years ago In Xueshan Village of Changping District in southwest Beijing and 40 kilometers from the city centre, signs of ancient human activity were discovered in the 1960s by archeologists, and a large amount of pottery was excavated. At that time, Beijing's weather was mild and humid, and the annual precipitation was approximately 100-200 mm—more than nowadays. This was the time period during which the Giza pyramids were built in the suburbs of modern-day Cairo.

Western Zhou Dynasty: 3000 years ago The remains of the city of Ji were discovered in the early 1960s in the modern-day Liulihe, a town located in southwest Beijing's Fangshan District, and 40 kilometers from the city centre. The city wall stretches a total of 829 meters, and is about 1 meter high. Palace remains have also been found within the city.

The Dabaotai Han Tomb is one of the main relics of the Han Dynasty in Beijing.

The 5th Century B.C. The small northern country of Yan set up it's capital in the city of Ji. Later on, the city of Ji moved to Guang'anmen, near the centre of modern-day Beijing. Ancient palace tile was discovered at this site during the 1950s. The city of Ji remained an important town of Beijing until the Qin Dynasty (221 B.C.-206 B.C.)—China's first Dynasty, founded by Emperor Chin Shihuang, who ordered the building of the Great Wall in the mountainous region to the north of Beijing.

Han Dynasty (206 B.C.-220 A.D.) When the ancestors of the Finnish, Estonian and Hungarian peoples were defeated by the Hans and migrated to Europe, the population of Beijing was about 50,000-60,000. A famous discovery was made when modern archaeologists unearthed a Han tomb in Dabao Village of Beijing's Fengtai District. By the time of the Tang Dynasty (618 A.D.-907 A.D.), when the Silk Road between China and Europe was established, the city of Ji had become the capital and political centre of the State of You. It continued to expand and grow with the passage of time. Up until the present time, more than 200 pottery wells have been discovered here.

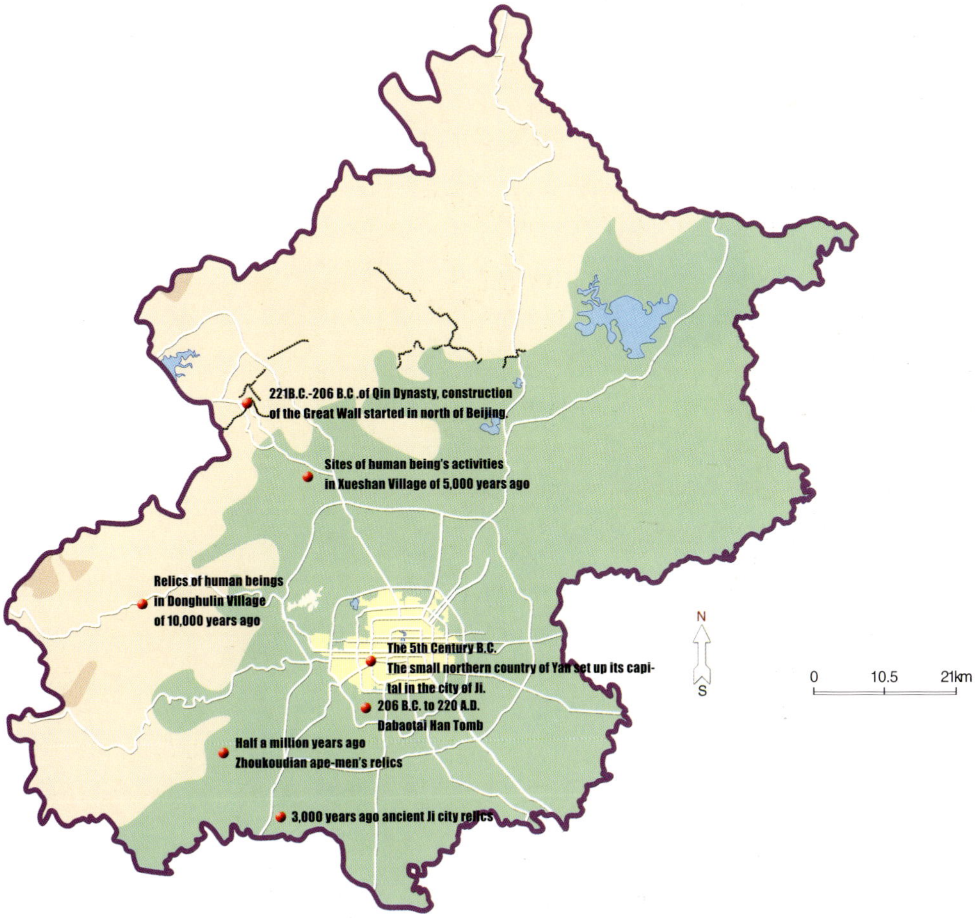

Historical relics of Beijing

The Lotus Pool today – the pool has shrunk considerably in size. Though much smaller than the past, the water lilies that grace its surface reflect the beauty and greatness of the Jin Dynasty.

2. After becoming the capital

In 938 A.D. the city of Ji became co-capital of the Liao Dynasty (916 -1125). And Beijing became a capital for the first time, with a population around 150,000.

In 1151 A.D. the Jin Dynasty (1115-1234) in northern China founded its capital in Beijing, choosing for its centre the Lotus Pool in western Xuanwu District. Many natural springs flowed in Beijing at the time, trees and grass flourished, which made for an excellent ecosystem. The city of Ji was square, with an area of 22 square kilometers, a perimeter of 18.7 kilometers, and a total of 12 city gates. Some names of the city gates are still in use today. Built on a grand scale, Its the palace has more than 600 buildings perimeter was 4.5 kilometers. By the time Paris was built and became the centre of northern France, Beijing's population had grown to around 400 thousand.

In 1260 the Mongol emperor Kublai Khan (reigned 1260-1294), grandson of the great Genghis Khan whose armies had marched all the way to far-off Europe, became the emperor of the Yuan Dynasty (1271-1368). He ordered the construction of his palace 5 kilometers to the northeast of the capital of Jin in 1261, the centre of the palace being on the site of the White Pagoda of today's Beihai Park. The length from east to west was 1,000 meters, and from north to south measured 740 meters with an area of 74 hectares, 4 times the area of the Louvre (not including the Tuileries Garden). The palace was called Yuan Dadu and was completed in 1272. As a result of the increase in population and the consequent necessary expansion'moving the city became a primary concern. Water shortage led the people to start making use of the abundant resources of the Gaoliang River in the north of the city. The chief designer of the magnificent palace was Liu Bingzhong (1216-1274). In 1275, Emperor Kublai Khan met the famous merchant Marco Polo (about 1254-1324) from Venice of Italy. Legend has it that he carried Chinese noodles back to Italy.

The Yuan Capital (Yuan Dadu) looked something like a large broad square. From north to south it measured 6,700 meters and 7,600 meters from east to west, covering about 51 square kilometers, equal in size to the modern city of Paris. Its wall was 16 meters in height, with a perimeter of 28.6 kilometers. During its most prosperous period, Yuan Dadu was a bustling city with 950 thousand people. The city was destroyed in 1368 when the Yuan Dynasty was overthrown. Gradually, it turned into a wasteland. Today, all that is left are some mud wall remains near the Second Ring Road of northwest Beijing.

Site of Yuan Dadu. The palace has disappeared, only a soil wall remains. Can you imagine how magnificent it must have been?

Stone carving of Kublai Khan

Stone carving of women dancers from the Yuan Dynasty

There are more than 8,700 rooms in the Forbidden City. From this bird's eye view, how many rooms can you see?

The old city wall of Beijing is not as sturdy as it was in the past, but it is witness to the past history.

In 1406 emperor Zhu Di (reigned 1403-1424) of the Ming Dynasty (1368-1644) started to construct a palace to the south of Yuan Dadu. When his palace—the Forbidden City—was finally completed, it was grand indeed—stretching 980 meters from north to south and 800 meters from east to west, surrounded by a moat, and having a total area of 78 hectares. In 1420, construction on the Inner and Outer cities was completed, with a total length of 10.8 kilometers, width of 7 kilometers, and an area of 57 kilometers. The circumference of the Forbidden City was 39.8 kilometers, with a moat encircling it. Sitting on the city wall was an observatory, its instruments

The ancient observatory built on the Jianguomen city wall of Beijing during the Zhengtong Years, the Ming Dynasty (1436 – 1449). The observatory is decorated by a dragon.

The moat outside Andingmen of the old Beijing city.

is made by bronze, the most advanced observatory of the time. Up until the middle of the 15th century, Chinese science and technology was first-rate in the world. The moat surrounding the Forbidden City had the functions of both protection and conveyance. The earliest water-route to encircle a city, it was a channel in harmony with nature. Currently the water quality is recovering. At that time, the peak population of Beijing amounted to 960 thousand. In 1421, the Ming Dynasty moved its capital to Beijing. Several years later, in 1487, primary construction was completed on the Russian city of Moscow. It wasn't until 1590 that the imperial palace was completed in Tokyo.

The bronze observatory

Dong Jiao Min Xiang. The building on the corner is from the time of William of Germany.After 1900, the area had been the Legation Quarter with foreign soldiers.

As a reminder of days gone by, the old Beijing railway station dates back to the era of British colonization, and it is similar to the Bombay Railway Station in India.

The Qing Dynasty founded in 1644 (1644-1911), adopted the Capital and Forbidden City of the Ming Dynasty. The Qing rulers built many mansions for relatives of the royal family, for example Yonghegong and Prince Gong's Mansion. Many gardens were also constructed in the suburbs, such as the Summer Palace and Yuanmingyuan. In later years of the Qing Dynasty, European style architecture started to spring up, like the foreign embassy district in Dong Jiao Ming Xiang, Catholic churches and the old Beijing railway station. Around this time the population was close to 800 thousand. In 1664, New York had just received its formal name, but it was only a small town of about a thousand people.

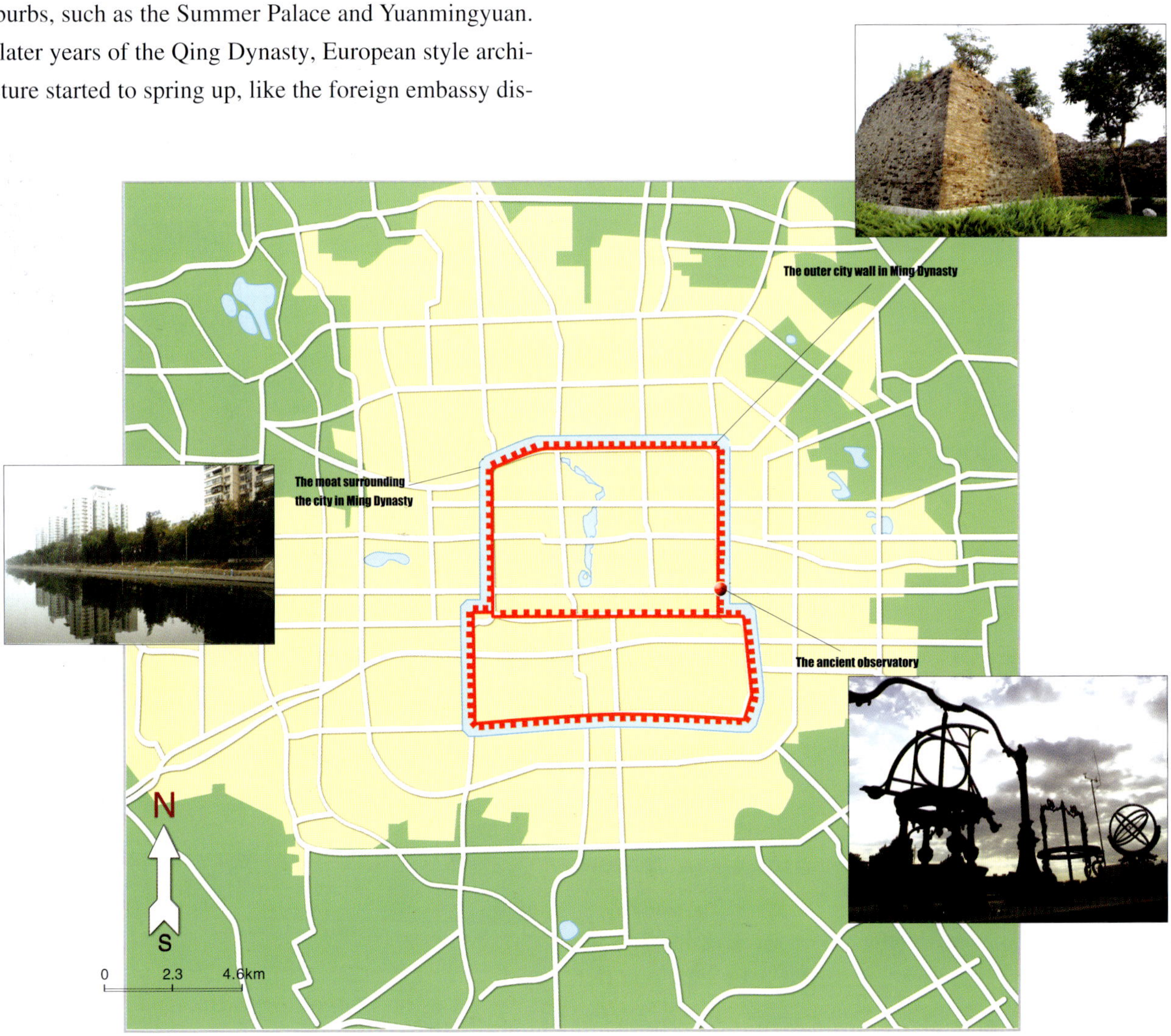

Positions of city wall, ancient observatory and moat

The European-style ruins at Yuanmingyuan

This diagram depicts the changes the capital has under gone over time.

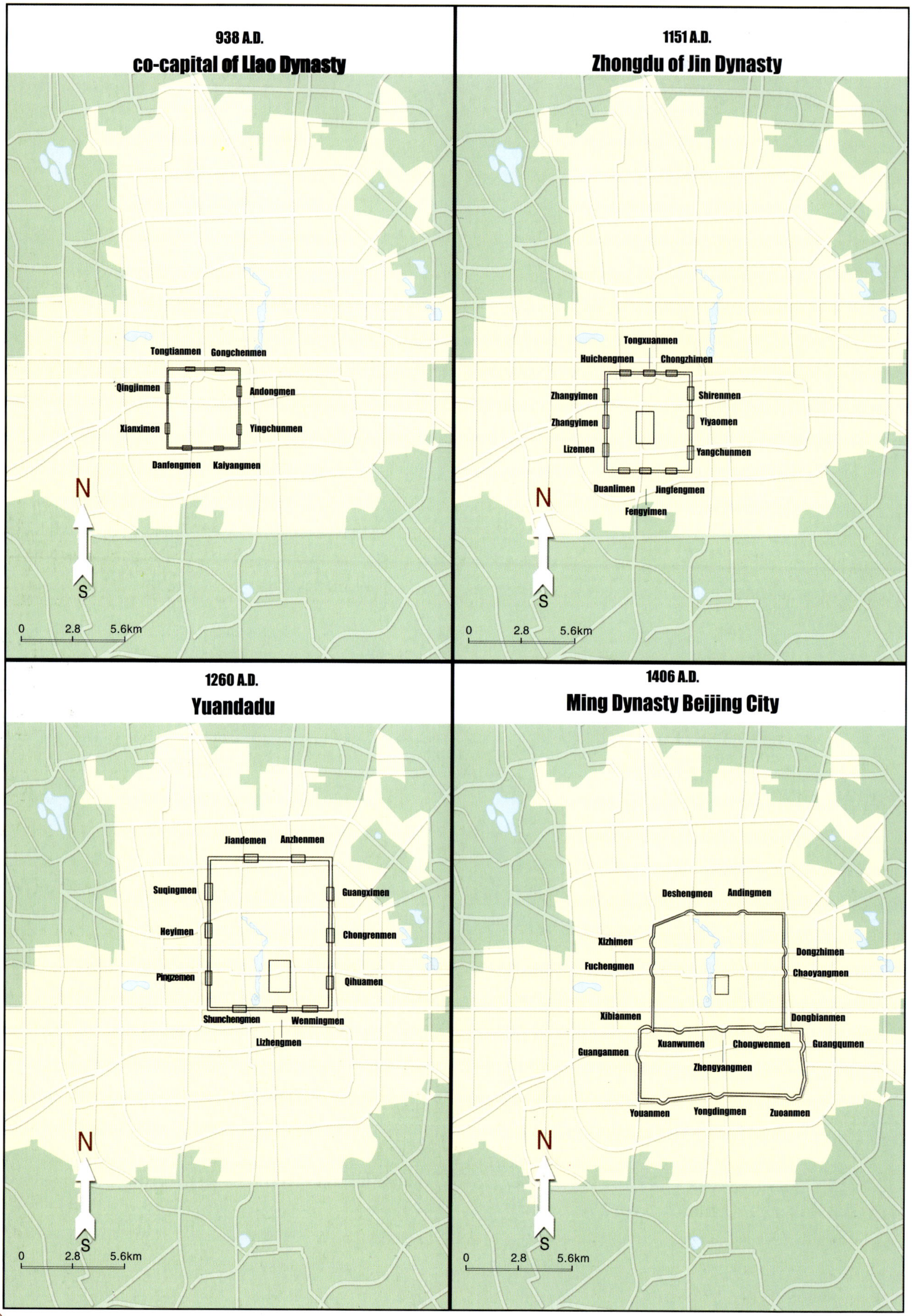

Lugou Bridge, built in 1189. Though today it stands in peace. The bullet marks in stone lions remind us the war of resistance.

There are 485 stone lions on the railings of Lugou Bridge. Can you count all of them?

The Republic of China (1912-1949) moved its capital to Nanjing. Except for few European style architecture, there was not really any large-scale construction to speak of in Beijing. On the 7th of July 1937, the Japanese began to invade China. That was the famous Lugou Bridge Incident. The population of Beijing at the time was around 1.5 million.

The stele of Lugouxiaoyue

The moment after Beijing officially won the right to host the 2008 Olympics. This was the first picture broadcasted by most of the major media after the decision of the 2001 Moscow International Olympic committee conference was announced. I am the first person on the left.

Tian'anmen Tower

The Olympic Countdown Clock in front of China's National Museum next to Tian'anmen Square.

In 1949 when the People's Republic of China was founded, the population of Beijing was around two million. Tian'anmen Square was expanded, and such structures as the Great Hall of the People and the Monument to the People's Heroes were built.

Since the Reform and Opening up of China **in 1978**, great changes have taken place in Beijing. Though more than half of the old districts have been removed, some traditional cultural areas have been retained. Grand architecture like The National Grand Theatre has been under construction. Beijing will be holding the 2008 Olympics. I was honored continuelly to make my contributions to Bejing Olympic Game.

3. Layout of Beijing

Beijing is a marvelous city, a representative of the diversity of world architecture. The general layout of Beijing is similar to that of Paris. Beijing takes Qian Men (the Front Gate) , Tian'anmen Square and the Forbidden City as the north-to-south axis, while Paris takes Notre Dame, the Louvre and the Arch of Triumph as the east-to-west axis, and both Beijing and Paris have city walls. Similar to New York, Beijing is a city artificially planed and constructed. There are streets numbered from south to north in New York; so it is with Dongsi, Dongdan, Xisi and Xidan of Beijing. In Tokyo of Japan, many buildings imitate the style of Beijing in various aspects. As a result, the style of Tokyo's ancient architecture mirrors that of Beijing. The imperial mausoleum in the suburbs of Beijing can only be matched by what is near Cairo, Egypt. The pyramids are above ground, while the Ming Tombs are under ground. Beijing's expanded Tian'anmen Square to a greater or lesser extent shows the influence of Red Square in Moscow. Not only is Beijing a historical city, but it is also a city in close relation with the world's cultures—a city that is developing along with world trends. Beijing is an energetic and innovative city. This is the most important reason why I want to show you around Beijing.

Culture Heritages in Beijing

The construction of the inner and outer cities was basically completed in the year 1420. All of the main historical and cultural heritages sites of Beijing can be found within this area, including sites constructed during the period of the establishment of the city. Old Beijing is the region inside the former city wall—that is the region inside today's Second Ring Road. On this point, Beijing is also similar to Paris. Old Paris refers to the region inside the former city wall, or the region within today's Ring Road (Boulevard Peripherique).

The north gate of the Forbidden City, which is now China's largest museum.

The moat of the Forbidden City and the Cape building hides mystery.

1. The Forbidden City

The Forbidden City (the Palace Museum) is on the World Heritage List. Lying in the west-central section of Beijing's Dongcheng District, it is Beijing's most famous cultural site. Its construction took 15 years. It began in 1406, and received its finishing touches in 1420, while the construction of the Louvre took about 500 years, from the 13th to the 18th centuries. Buildings within the Forbidden City are wood structures, as opposed to the stone architecture of the Louvre. As a result, the difficulty of the project was slightly less than that of the Louvre. However, it was still no easy project, standing as a monument to the huge manpower and vast material resources of the Ming Dynasty. The Louvre takes buildings as its outermost protecting structures, whereas the Forbidden City is surrounded by a moat 52 meters in breadth. The Forbidden City is 950 meters long from north to south and 756 meters wide from east to west, covering 72 hectares, which is 4 times the area of the Louvre (not including the Tuileries Garden). The number of rooms in the Forbidden City is more than 8,700, with a total floor space of 150,000 square meters. Over a period of 500 years, a total of 24 emperors ascended the throne here.

My family moved to Beijing from Chongqing in 1946. Our first residence was less than 200 meters from the Forbidden City. Later we moved only 100 meters closer to the Forbidden City—both within the bounds of the original emperor's city. Nearly every day I saw the Cape Building of the Forbidden City in that time. In my childhood, I sensed the magnificent splendor of the grand Forbidden City, and listened to many a mysterious story from its ancient days. Later on in life, I got to enjoy the view of the Eiffel Tower from my residence in Paris.

The Hall of Preserving Harmony was a piece of exquisite imperial architecture, with 10 pillars in front and 9 rooms.

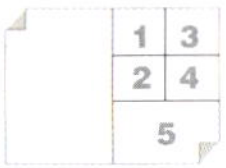

1 The interior of the Hall of Preserving Harmony. The plaque is carved with the four words "Huang Jian You Ji", meaning that the standard is set according to the behavior of the emperor.

2 A plaque bearing the inscription, "Be open and aboveboard", enumerating the qualities of integrity that an ideal emperor should possess.

3 Outside the gate of the Hall of Mental Cultivation.

4 Are the decorations in the Hall of Mental Cultivation a little feminized?

Moving from south to north along the middle axis of the Forbidden City, we can find three grand palaces: The Hall of Supreme Harmony, also called Jinluan Palace—this is where the emperor ascended the throne. Built in 1420, the hall is 35 meters high, covers 2,377square meters (two thirds the size of Notre Dame). Next comes the Hall of Complete Harmony followed by the Hall of Preserving Harmony. The Hall of Preserving Harmony is where banquets were held in honor of aristocrats and high-ranking officials. It is also the place where China's old civil service examination was held.

There are three more palaces at the north end of the middle axis line: The Palace of Heavenly Purity (built in 1420), The Hall of Union and Peace (rebuilt in 1978) and The Palace of Earthly Tranquility (rebuilt in 1655). These places are where the emperor worked, performed ceremonies and resided. Meridian Gate is the main gate of the Forbidden City. Located on the south end of the Forbidden City, it was built in 1420, 35.6 meters in height. It is composed of a large tower with four pavilions on each side, known as the "Five Phoenix Tower". Three impressive gates open through the middle of the tower with smaller side doors positioned to the right and left. With its golden tiles and red walls, Meridian Gate looks really magnificent. There is a broad square in front of the gate, here the emperor held many a grand ceremony.

Another one of the most important buildings in the Forbidden City is the Hall of Mental Cultivation, built in 1420. It was here that Empress Dowager Cixi (1861-1908) carried out the practice of "holding court behind a screen". (She would sit behind Emperor Guanxu, the two of them separated by a screen. From this hidden vantage point she would tell the emperor what to follow—an artful control of power, indeed.)

What do you feel as you stand in front of Meridian Gate? Grandeur or repression? Praise or disappointment? It all depends on your value system. But one thing is for sure—you can't ignore it, for it is history.

It could be said that if you can find a dark corner in the Louve at sunset, then you can find such a place in the Forbidden City in broad daylight. That's why it is an imperial palace.

The Shadow Wall is a unique form of Chinese architecture, protecting the privacy of inner rooms. It is a common sight in the palace.

The Cape Tower that connects the main halls is resplendent as well.

Compared with the large Forbidden City, Emperor Qianlong's Garden is smaller and more delicate.

The place where Zhenfei was drowned – the well of Zhenfei records the story of an age.

The photo of Zhenfei

The Forbidden City is similar to the Louvre, but different from the imperial palaces of Tokyo and Seoul in that it is characterized by architecture as opposed to gardens. The Imperial Garden of the Forbidden City-The garden of Emperor Qianlong's was only 0.6 hectares in size. Nevertheless it boasts a variety of architectural styles and is filled with a profound palace atmosphere, while adorned by ancient trees and rare flowers. Like many palaces in the world, there are tragic stories of queens and imperial concubines in the Forbidden City. One of the saddest is that of Qing Emperor Guangxu's (reigned 1875-1908) favorite concubine, known as Zhenfei, who was dropped down a narrow well under the order of the Empress Dowager Cixi in 1900.

Flying dragon stone carving. Such intricately designed stairs are rare in the world.

1 The copper lion before the palace of Heavenly Purity.

2 This gold-plated copper vat makes use of rain water.

3 "Sun clock" – the stone sundial.

4 Copper censer with stone platform.

5 Red painted doors with eight rows of nine golden knobs each, totaling 72 golden knobs can only be found in the imperial palaces.

6 Copper censer with stone platform(circular).

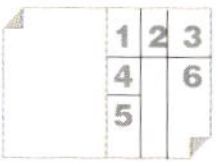

Besides the magnificent architecture of the Forbidden City, there are many other exquisite sculptures and noteworthy objects. There are red painted gates with golden knobs, stone stairways accompanied by large stone reliefs. In front of the stairs and beside the door, there used to be copper lions, an ancient Chinese sundial, a large vat that collected rainwater for fire protection and an incense burner.

In the magnificent and ornate Forbidden City, you will walk in the footsteps of the founder of Ming Dynasty, Emperor Zhu Di. Have you ever realized that at the beginning of the century when Columbus found a new sea-lane, Emperor Zhu Di constructed the largest ever imperial palace, set up the largest ever planned city, as well as built the world's first large-scale fleet of ocean-going vessels? Have you ever stopped to wonder why his work was not carried on?

The Forbidden City is different from the Louvre in that you cannot smoothly course your way through from one part to the next. Rather, since it is divided into many smaller courtyards of different sizes, you must plan your route in advance, so as not to neglect any important spots. To put it in simple words, the Forbidden City (from 1925 it has been know as the world famous Palace Museum) is simply too large to see all in one day. On a daily basis, only certain parts are open to the public. A thorough visit may demand 2 or 3 days.

The Moat and the Cape Building

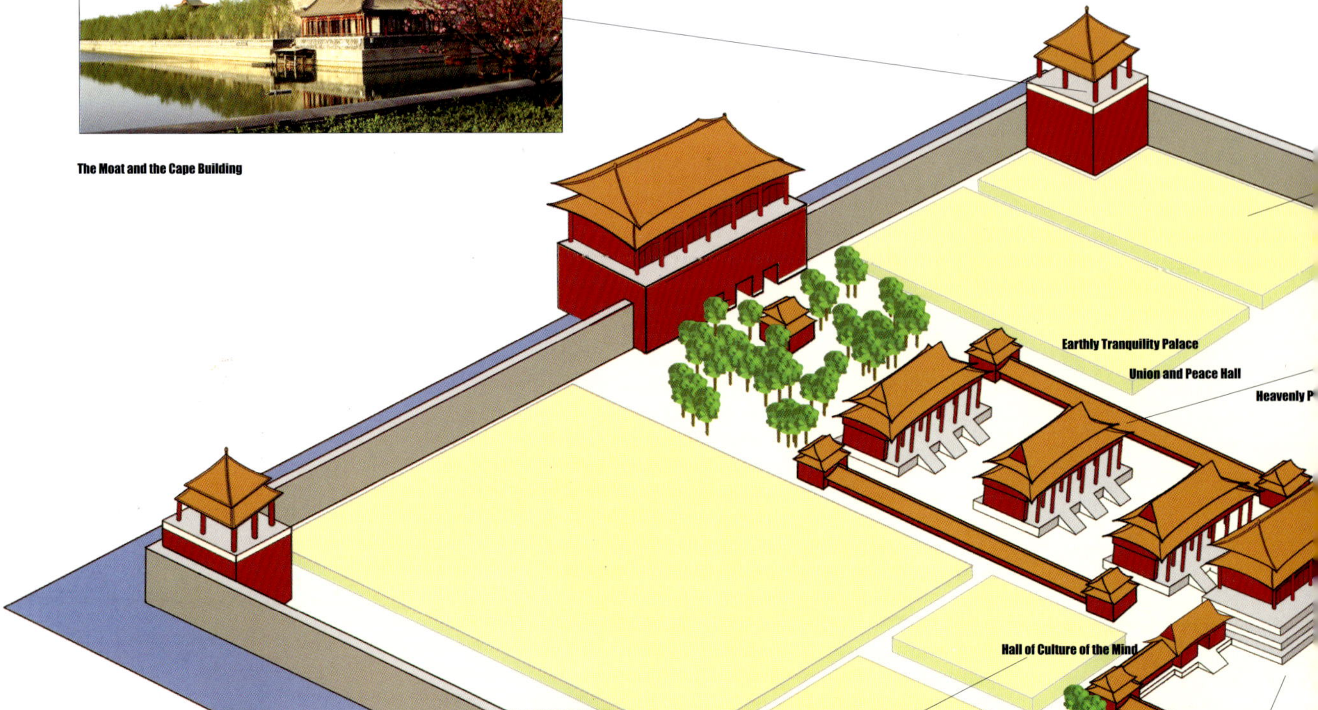

Out of the Gate of Hall of Culture of the Mind

Exterior of Preserving Harmony Hall

Qianlong's Garden

Heavenly Purity Palace

Supreme Harmony Hall

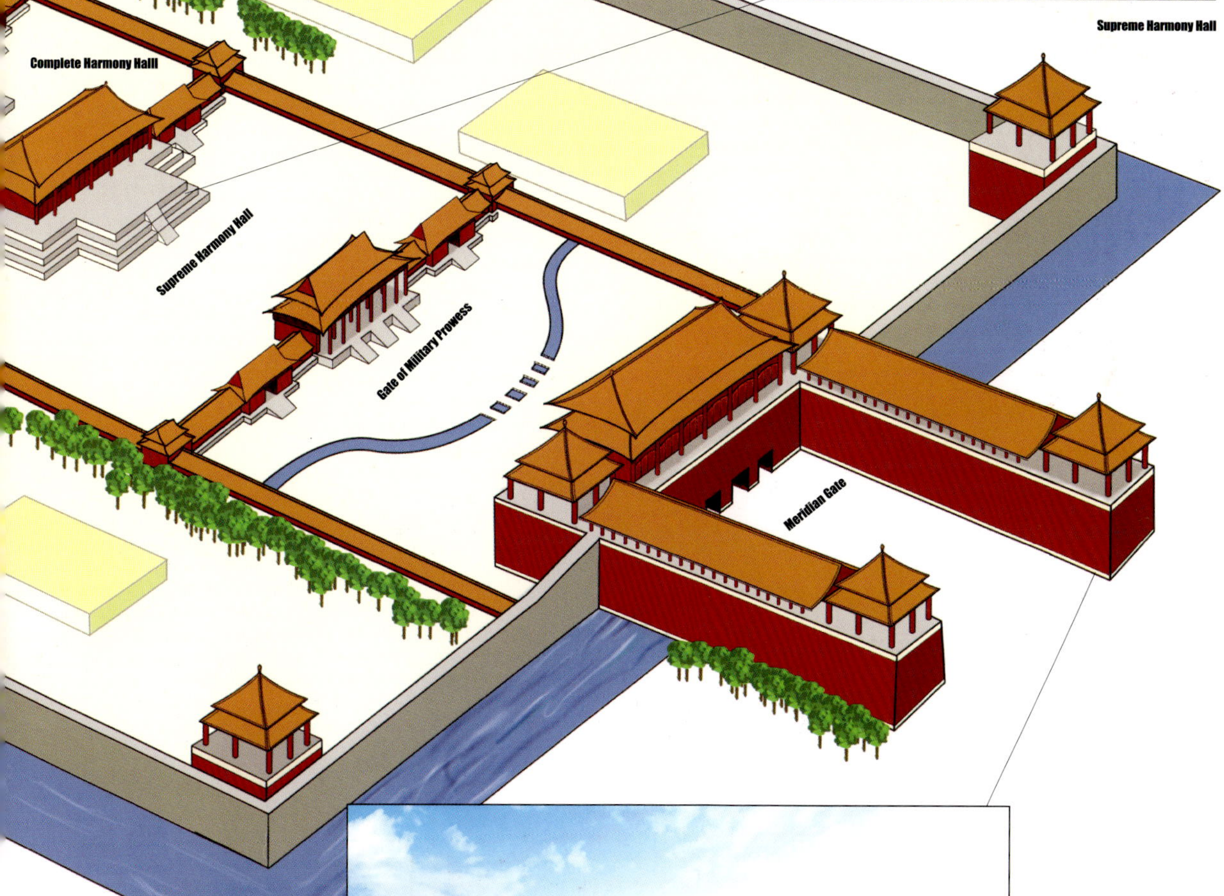

Exterior of Meridian Gate

Tian'anmen Tower, a building used for the inspection of troops and the holding of grand ceremonies.

2. Tian'anmen Square

Tian'anmen Square takes the former south gate of the Forbidden City as its north end. Its south end is the south gate of the old Inner city—Zhengyanmen. It was expanded to today's size step by step after the founding of the People's Republic of China in 1949. Today, Tian'anmen Square encompasses about 44 hectares which is 4 times the area of the Triumphal Arch Square, and twice as large as Moscow's Red Square. If the area of the street around is calculated, it is more than 70 hectares, which could hold an assembly of a million people at the same time. Chang'an Street, running from east to west at the north end of Tian'anmen Square, is the longest, widest and most important street in Beijing. It is 10 kilometers long and 120 meters wide, 2 kilometers longer, and 1.6 times wider than Champs Elysees.

Tian'anmen (meaning the "Gate of Heavenly Peace") is the square's most important piece of architecture. Built in 1417, the gate is 33.7 meters in height, standing a little lower than the Parisian Arch of Triumph (which is 50 meters high). Tian'anmen is used for the inspection of troops, and it is one of only a few "triumphal arches" which differs from the Roman style. Tian'anmen witnessed the last century of Chinese history. It was here, on October 1, 1949, that Chairman Mao, one of the important founders of the People's Republic of China, proclaimed its establishment to the world. As mentioned above, the south end of the square is guarded by Zhengyangmen, also named Qianmen (Front Gate). It was built in 1421 and is about 42 meters high. In front of it stands the Arrow Tower, set up in 1439 as a defense against enemies.

Tian'anmen Square is similar to Moscow's Red Square. Not only is it close to government office buildings, but it is also surrounded by many spots of interest.

The Monument to the People's Heroes was built in the middle of Tian'anmen Square. Erected in April of 1958 using a total of 17 thousand white marble and granite bricks, it stands 37.94 meters in height. It was constructed in memory of the martyrs who laid down their lives for the revolutionary struggle of the Chinese people from 1840 to 1949. There are white marble reliefs at the base of the monument depicting key episodes of the Chinese struggle for freedom and independence. On the west side of Tian'anmen Square is the Great Hall of the People, set up in 1959. It is the meeting place for the National People's Congress—National Parliament. The floor space is 171,000 square meters, which is more than that of the Forbidden City. The central hall is 76 meters long and 60 meters wide, with an area of 4,600 square meters, almost equal to the area of St. Peter's Basilica in Rome. In the south part of Tiananmen Square lies Chairman Mao's (1893-1976) Memorial Hall, built in 1977. Here are the remains of Mao Ze Dong, lying reclined in a crystal coffin to be paid respects to.

Five-Starred Red Flag flicking on the Tian'anmen Square and national flag's guardian

The south gate of the inner Beijing City – Zhengyangmen, namely the Front Gate, was built in 1421 and is 42 meters high.

The Arrow Tower was built in 1439. It has 82 windows from which arrows could be shot in defense of Qian Men (the Front Gate).

1 The Great Hall of the People is the meeting place for National People's Congress.

2 Tian'anmen Square is about 1,000 meters long from south to north, and 700 meters from east to west, with a total area of 70 hectares, and is one of the largest city squares in the world.

3 Monument to the People's Heroes.

1 Like the Vendome in Paris and the Ayuwang pillars in Nepal, the Marble Pillars, were set up for commemorative purposes. From the tops of the pillars an imaginary beast called "Hou" looks off into the distance, off toward the emperor's residence.

2 The National Museum of China.

3 The National Grand Theater will be open in 2007.

In 2006, The National Grand Theatre was built to the west of the Great Hall of the People. It is completely modern, which is designed by a French architect. The theatre has added a modern flavor to old Tian'anmen Square. What effect will this have on the former style of Beijing? We'd love to know what you think once you've seen it.

Monument of the People's Heros

Tian'anmen Tower

The right one is Zhengyangmen and the left one is Arrow Tower

Imperial's Garden – Taiye Lake and the White Pagoda of Nepalese Style erects on Qionghua Island.

The Five-Dragon Pavilions resemble five pavilion boats bearing up to the Forbidden City.

3. Beihai Park

Beihai Park (North Sea) lies just 100 meters to the west of the Coal Park. Originally, it was also a private garden of the imperial family, with an area of 68.2 hectares. It is similar to Luxemburg Park of Paris or Central Park in New York City, while it differs from the foregoing in that its main scenery is water. A man-made lake — Taiye Lake (also known as Beihai) —is at the centre of the park, with a total area of 38.9 hectares. This lake was once the centre of the Yuandadu Palace. In the middle of the lake is Qionghua Island (also called as Baita Hill), on which in the year 1651, a Nepalese style stupa was erected. It is known as the White Pagoda, and stands 35.9 meters high. As a youngster, I would go boating on this lake. I couldn't help thinking to myself: it is truly an earthly heaven.

On the north bank of Taiye Lake, you can find the famous Five-Dragon Pavilions. Built in 1602, the Five Pavilions stand along the lake as if they were pavilion boats being pushed along in the breeze. Another noteworthy spot is the Nine-Dragon Screen built in 1756 on the north side of the lake. It stretches 25.9 meters in length and is 6.6 meters high and 1.4 meters thick. The double-sided wall is covered with colored glazed tiles, which make nine different dragons of striking appearance. The dragon is a mythological animal in the ancient Chinese tradition. It symbolizes the ancestors and imperial power of the Chinese.

Detail of the Nine-Dragon Screen

Nine-Dragon Screen – a symbol of the majesty and power of China. Nine dragons slither across the highest part of the dragon screen. In all, the screen has 135 dragons.

To the west of Beihai Park's south gate is a small and delicate park known as the Round City. You can't miss it! Only 4,500 square meters in size, it is surrounded by a 4.6-meter high circular wall and has a distinctive courtyard with hallsand pavilions. The ancient trees here have gained life-giving water from a water-channel system for the last 500 years—an amazing "irrigation" technique. Though its height is only one fifth of the ancient Hanging Gardens of Babylon, it is magnificent indeed.

The Round City under a blue sky

Five-Dragon Pavilions

Nine-Dragon Screen

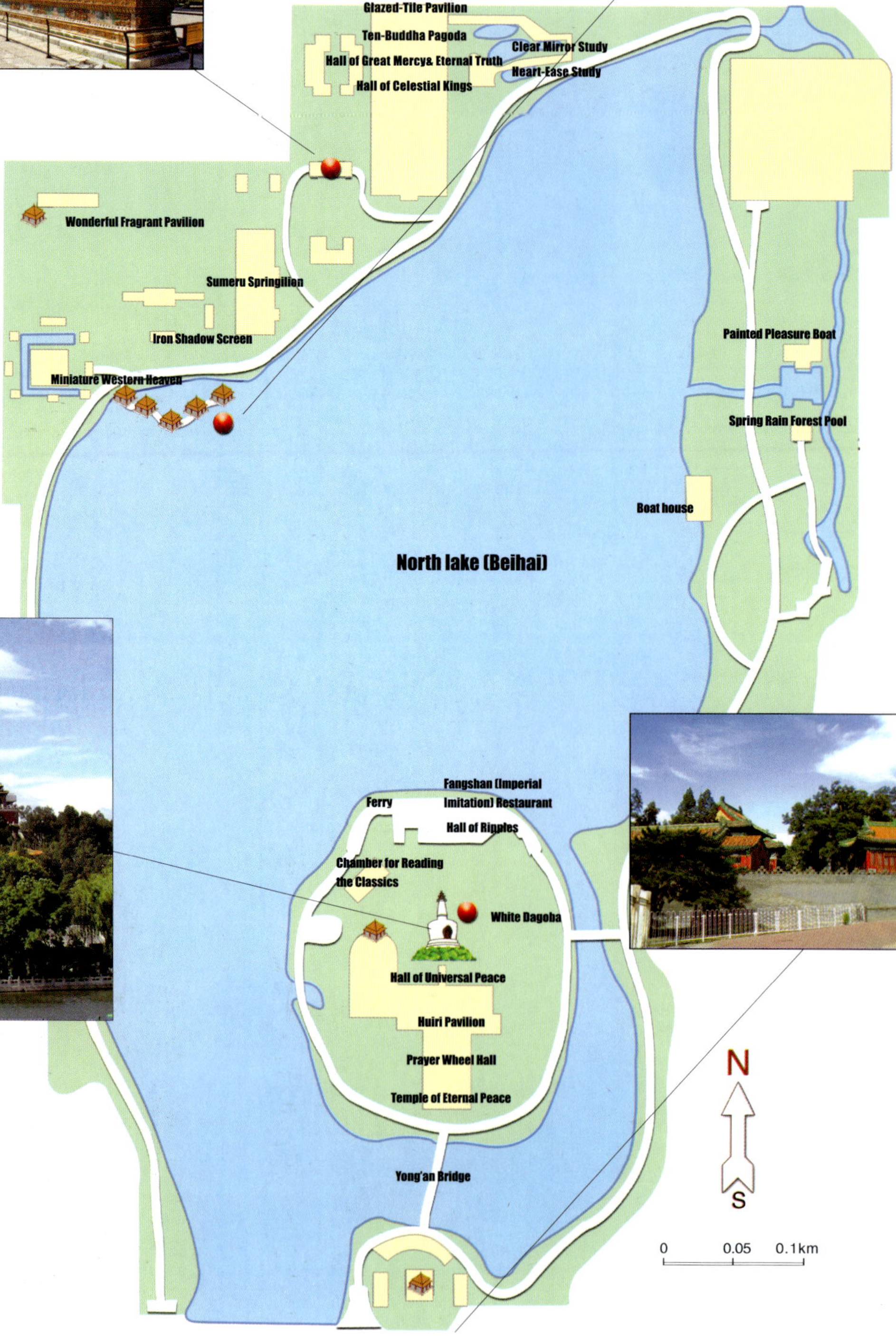

Taiye Lake and Jade Floery Isle

Round City

The front gate of Coal Hill Park

4. Coal Hill Park

Coal Hill Park lies right to the north of the Palace Museum. It used to be a private garden of the imperial family. Wansui Hill rises in the centre of the park. Wansui Hill is also known as Coal Hill, as it is made up of coal and left-over dirt from ancient construction projects. It is a 600-year-old example of waste-removal. In 2000, I suggested that a similar "waste material hill"be set up at the north end of the same meridian line in the new Olympic Park. These two hills could sit facing each other, each silently witnessing how humanity has changed over the last six centuries. Coal Hill is 50 meters high, with five small peaks. During the Qing dynasty, pavilions were built on each of the five peaks. The one in the middle is called Everlasting Spring Pavilion.

In 1644, when a peasant army led by Li Zicheng broke into Beijing, the last Ming Emperor Chongzhen hung himself from a tree in Coal Hill Park, marking the end of the Ming Dynasty. The position of Coal Hill Park in Beijing is somewhat similar to Montmartre of Paris—it could have a bird's eye view of Beijing. However, it is not a place where artists live. To the north of Coal Hill Park is the children's palace, a club that trains artists and athletes. The world's first Chinese table tennis champion, as well as many famous artists, were trained here. Half a century ago, I had my happy childhood here in Coal Hill Park.

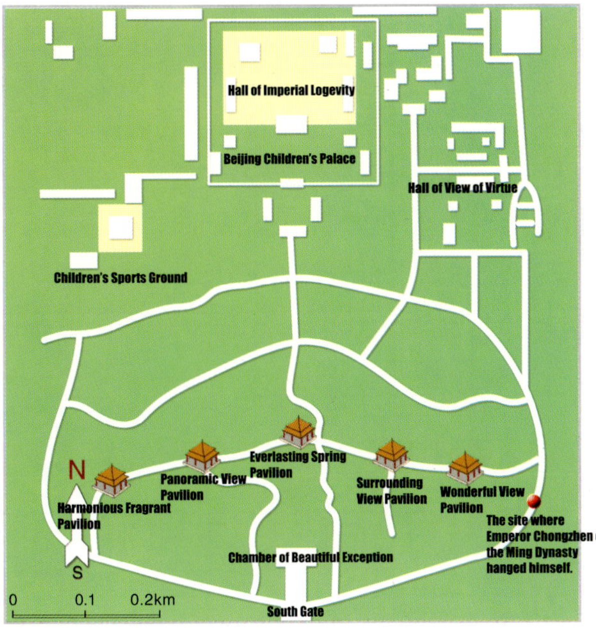

The Beijing Children's Palace, located at Coal Park, cultivates many young talents.

The tree where Emperor Chongzhen hanged himself.

祈年殿

The Circular Mound Altar was built in 1530. It was the main place where the emperor offered sacrifices to the god of heaven. The number of columns and stairs is multiples of nine, which was considered a "positive number".

◀The Hall of Prayer for Good Harvests is one of the symbols of Beijing.

The Imperial Vault to the north of the Circular Mound Altar is the place where the tablets of gods were kept.

5. The Temple of Heaven

The Chinese emperors used to place more importance on the worship of heaven than on Buddhism, especially after the Ming and Qing Dynasties. For them, offering sacrifices to the god of heaven corresponded to church going. The times of offering sacrifices to heaven were less frequent than church-going, but the occasion was nonetheless magnificent. Located in Chongwen District (part of the Outer City), with a total area of 273 hectares, the Temple of Heaven is the biggest park in downtown, which corresponds to Notre

Gate of the Hall of Abstinence

Dame in Paris. It is also a symbol of Beijing, and a part of the world heritages.

The Hall of Prayer for Good Harvests is the main structure in the compound. It is a lofty cone-shaped building located in the northern end of the park. It was built in 1420. The entire structure is 38.0 meters high and 37.7 meters in diameter, covering about 1,100 square meters. The Circular Mound Altar is where the emperor offered sacrifices to the god of heaven. It was built in 1530—a three-layer platform made of white marble forming a total of nine stages. To the north of Circular Mound Altar lies the Imperial Vault of Heaven, also built in 1530, and it's where the so-called tablets of the gods were placed. A circular wall encloses the Imperial Vault of Heaven. Since the wall is extremely smooth, speaking close to it will create an echo. Thus it is known as "The Echo Wall". The Hall of Abstinence is located in the south of the park. This was the place where the emperors used to hold ceremonial fasts when offering sacrifices to god. The Hall of Abstinence contains five bedrooms and a bell tower.

Hall of Prayer Good Harvests

Echo Wall

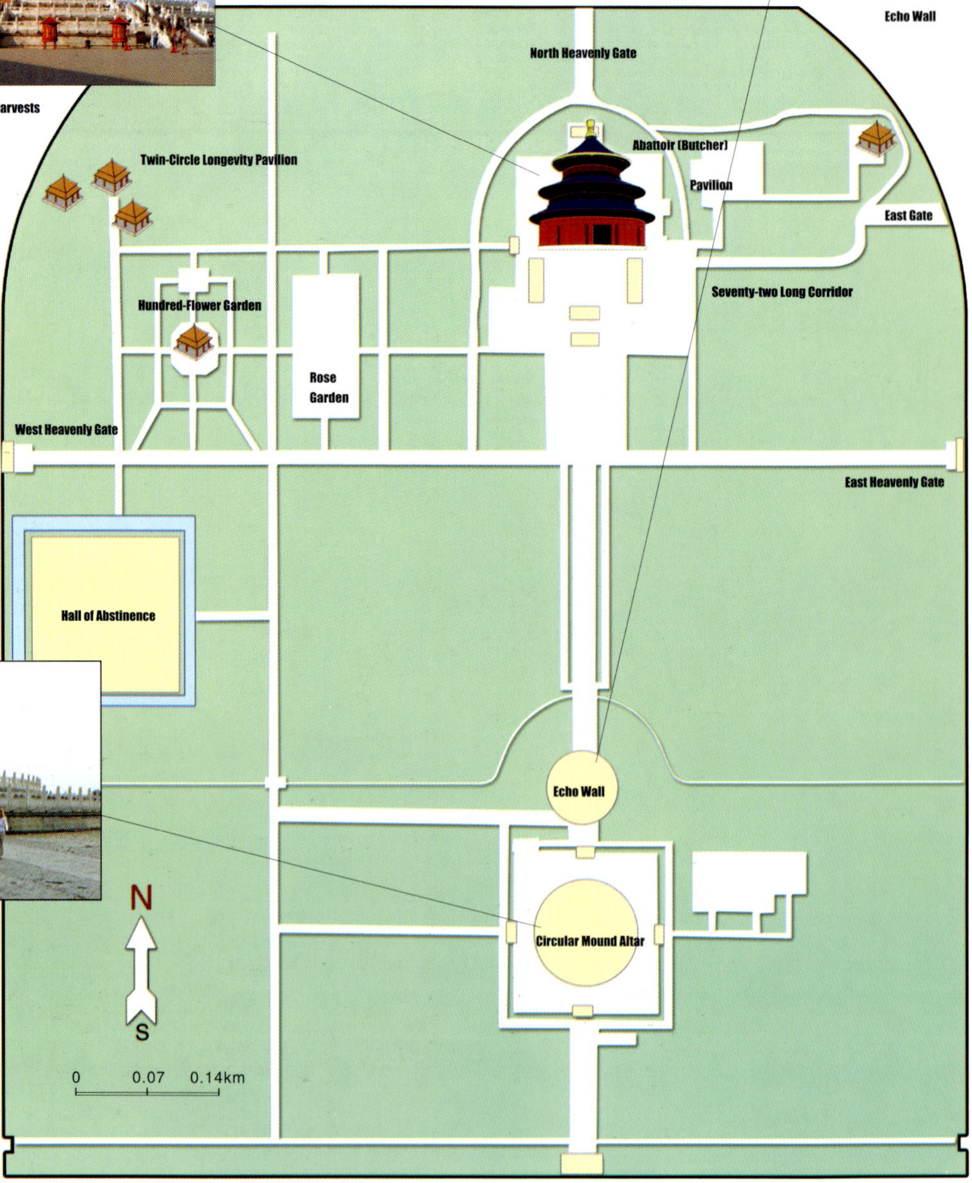

Circular Mound Altar

6. The Princes' Mansion

In the early history of China, the centralization of power had already been carried out .After the Qing Dynasty, nobility in China were different from that of France who constructed their mansions outside the capital or in the suburbs. Chinese nobility were required to build theirs in the city. Therefore, here in Beijing there are fabulous mansions that could rival the imperial palace in beauty. Prince Gong's Mansion (residence of the last Qing emperor's father) is a good example. Built in 1789, the mansion is among those who are exquisitely decorated in the world.

Prince Gong's Mansion —the cuijin Garden covers an area of 2.5 hectares.

Prince Gong's Mansion is regarded as the inspiration of the great work *Dream of the Red Chamber.* This picture shows a corridor in Prince Gong's Mansion.

Culture Heritages in the Suburbs of Beijing

The city of Beijing has been formed gradually over the past 3, 000 years. Its location within the region has changed over time. As a result, many culture heritage sites can be found in the suburbs of Beijing.

Florid night of the Great Wall

The Ming Tombs

The Summer Palace

The front gate of the Summer Palace

1. The Summer Palace

The world's gardens could be classified into five kinds: the French, Chinese, English, Arabian and Japanese types. The Summer Palace is a typical Chinese Garden. Here within its walls can be found a "garden within a garden". The Garden of Harmonious Interest is the prototype of Japanese gardens. The hill behind it is mainly covered by natural trees and plants, which is similar to English gardens. Zhongshan Park to the west of Tian'anmen shares features with the French garden style.

An imperial garden, the Summer Palace is one of the most famous four gardens of the Qing Dynasty to be found in Beijing. It is similar to Versailles in the outskirts of Paris (Versailles is called the Summer Palace as well), and is on the World Heritage list. The Summer Palace is located in the northwest of Beijing's Haidian District, 15 kilometers from the downtown, again similar to Versailles, which is 18 kilometers from Paris. Early in the first year of the Jin emperor Zhenyuan (1153), this spot was designated for the imperial palace; but a large-scale construction did not start until the Qing Dynasty. Construction began in 1705, and was completed by 1750. Destroyed by the Anglo-French Allied Forces in 1860, the Summer Palace was restored in 1888 by Empress Dowager Cixi, supported by funds intended for the development of the Navy. Its 290 hectares are roughly divided into two parts—Longevity Hill and Kunming Lake. Water accounts for two thirds of its area, the largest water-land ratio of any imperial gardens in the world. Kunming Lake differs from the lake behind Versailles in that there are many scenic spots along its banks.

Lions in front of the Gate of the Summer Palace

The Marble Boat, constructed by the Empress Dowager Cixi with funds intended for the development of the navy, is one of history's lesson books.

The inner garden – Garden of Harmonious Interest.

Longevity Hill never gave Empress Dowager Cixi long life; Off in the distance, the West Mountains are what is truly enduring. The highest monument anyone leave for himself is the maintaining of the ecosystem.

◀— Seventeen-Arch Bridge is a perfect combination of China's southern and northern bridge styles.

Longevity Hill sits to the north bank of Kunming Lake, a natural hill with the height of 108.9 meters. There was an ancient legend that told of an old man chiseling urns on this hill, and as a result the place became known as Weng (Urn) Hill. To wish Empress Dowager long life on her birthday, it was renamed Longevity Hill. The main building on the hill is the Tower of Buddhist Incense. On a 20 meters high platform, about 100 meters from the surface of the lake, the Tower is an eight-sided three-story building with four eaves, 41 meters in height. It is a good spot to get a general view of the western outskirts of Beijing.

Seventeen-Arch Bridge is the longest stone bridge in the garden. Built in the 1740s, the bridge connects the east bank of the lake and Southern Lake Island. It is 150 meters long with seventeen arches, a combination of both the southern and northern bridge styles of ancient China. There are 544 stone lions on the balusters of the bridge, each having a different expression.

The Marble Boat, built in 1755, also called Qingyanfang, is "anchored" at the western foot of Longevity Hill. Originally there was a Chinese style wooden superstructure on the top of it. In 1860, it was burned down by the Anglo-French forces. In 1893 it was restored to take the form of a foreign ship. The Boat was 36 meters long, with upper and lower levels. The cabin is made of wood, while the floor is paved with colored brick.

Built in 1751, the Garden of Harmonious Interest is located at the east foot of Longevity Hill. This is one of the famous "gardens within a garden". It is actually an imitation of Huishan Gardens in Southern China. "Moving southern scenery to the north" is the main purpose for the construction of the Summer Palace, a collection of best Chinese garden styles.

In another famous inner garden—the Garden of Virtuous Harmony could be found the largest opera house in China at that time.

雲輝玉宇

Built in 1891, the 3-level opera house is 21 meters high, the stage of which is 17 meters wide. It was here that famous artists would performe Beijing Opera as well as other forms of entertainment for the emperors and royalty.

Kunming Lake is at the foot of Longevity Hill. On the northern bank, there is one of the most delicate archways still extant in Beijing.

Different from the king of France who could look through the windows to the outside world, emperors in the Forbidden City and the Summer Palace were isolated by high walls. The Chinese emperors could not see their citizens, so Shopping Street was built along the Back Lake, imitating the shops along the canals in Suzhou. Eunuchs acted as the shop keepers at the time. The old man in the picture is selling Chinese calligraphy and other artwork.

In the year 1750, construction began on the Long Corridor. It lies along the northern shore of Kunming Lake and to the south of Longevity Hill. It is known as the longest painted corridor in the world —728 meters long with 273 sections. The beams of the corridor are decorated with more than 8,000 paintings of scenery, characters and tales, thus comes the name " painted corridor".

1 The theater building in the Garden of Virtuous Harmony. Why no hall for the audience? Because it belonged to the imperial family.

2 The " Yunhui Yuyu" Archways were designed as memorial structures, similar to the Arch of Triumph in Europe.

3 Suzhou Street – shopping street

4 An older man selling calligraphy

5 This fancy corridor is the longest art corridor in the world.

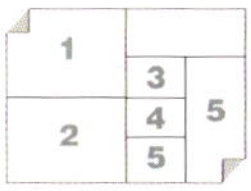

1 Kylin, the animal of Chinese fable

2 Copper censer

3 This peculiar stone collection is a kind of Chinese art. Like abstract sculpture, these stones give people an image of infinity. Isn't natural stone artwork more in harmony with nature? What do you think of these stones?

The Kylin is an animal in ancient Chinese mythology. A symbol of luck, the Kylin combines parts of many animals. It has a lion's head, deer's antlers, a horse's body, and fish scales. Nowadays, this dream may be realized through genetic engineering.

Almost anywhere in this beautiful garden, you can see the footsteps of the Empress Dowager Cixi. You are sure to question, how could a woman like Empress Dowager Cixi control such a great country as China for such a long period of time—for 47 years, from the middle of the 19th century to the beginning of the 20th century?

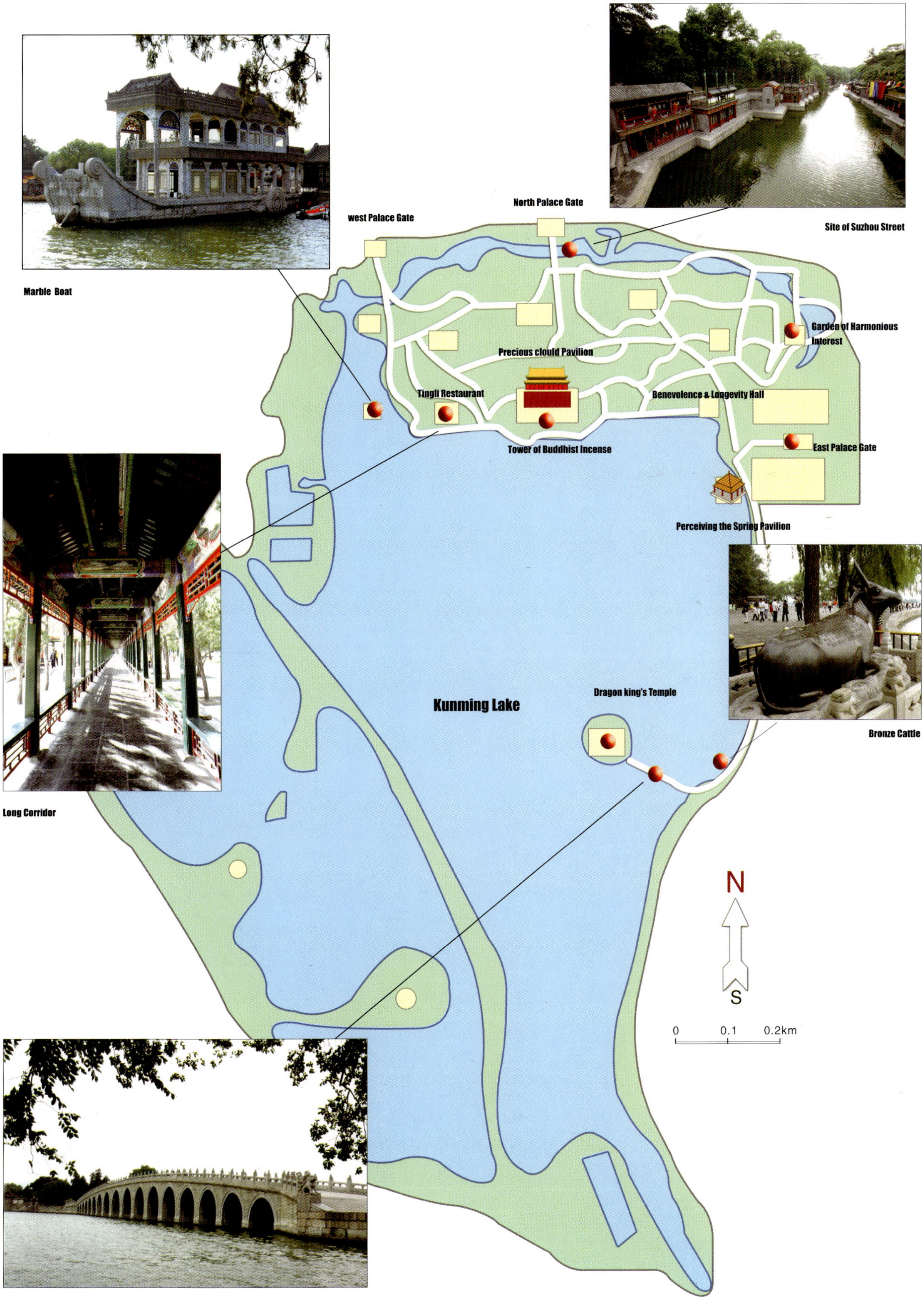

Marble Boat

Site of Suzhou Street

Long Corridor

Bronze Cattle

Seventeen-Arch Bridge

2. The Ruins of Yuanmingyuan

In the east of Beijing's Haidian District, and 1,000 meters to the northeast of the Summer Palace sits the former largest imperial garden in the world —Yuanmingyuan. It encompasses an area of 347 hectares with a water surface area of 140 hectares. It is more than 10 kilometers in length. The garden contains more than 100 scenic spots, and its floor space is 160,000 square meters, 10,000 square meters more than the Forbidden City, and 1.5 times that of Versailles (110,000 square meters). The project started in 1709 and was completed in 1744 by the strongest country of the time, the Qing Empire. Up until 1820, China's GNP was ranked number one in the world. Yuanmingyuan has four inner gardens: Yuanming, Changchun, Wanchun, and Yichun. Today's Peking University and Tsinghua University have incorporated parts of the former Yuanmingyuan.

Within the garden lake and hill, flower and forest interspersed beautifully with 145 different pavilions and buildings. Yuanmingyuan was also home to an imperial museum with a vast collection of invaluable cultural treasures. It was not only " a garden of gardens", but also a treasury of art. Designers such as the Italian missionary Boanerges Langshining (1688-1766) took part in the design of Da Shui Fa and other grand western buildings, which made Yuanmingyuan a garden with the combination of both eastern and western styles. Its scope is much larger than any of the " Chinese Palaces" to be found in the imperial gardens of Versailles, Potsdam, Stockholm or any other European imperial gardens, for that matter.

However, Yuanmingyuan was burned by French and British troops in 1860. 2,500 years ago, the Acropolis of Athens became ruins. The palaces of Ancient Rome became relics 1,500 years ago, and the Tuileries Garden of the Louvre came across the same fate 230 years ago. Finally, Yuanmingyuan—perhaps the last such monument of ancient civilization—was destroyed 150 years ago. Standing at the entrance to the Yuanmingyuan ruins at sunset, watching the resplendence of the western sky, you may feel that you have stepped back into the past history.

Should Yuanmingyuan be restored? This question is currently under hot discussion in Beijing. Neither the Acropolis nor the ancient Roman Palace has been restored. Having visited Yuanmingyuan, what do you think of the project? Fuhai (the Lake of Blessings) has been recovered. A major point of discussion has been whether or not the lake bottom should be lined with bricks. The present conclusion is to line the lake bottom with clay in order to reduce water leakage. This approach will spare the necessity of laying bricks, leaving the lake in its natural state. Of all the options, this plan is based on the most harmonious relationship between man and nature.

The ruins of Xiyanglou reflect history

The Lake of Blessings turned into paddy field a hundred years ago.

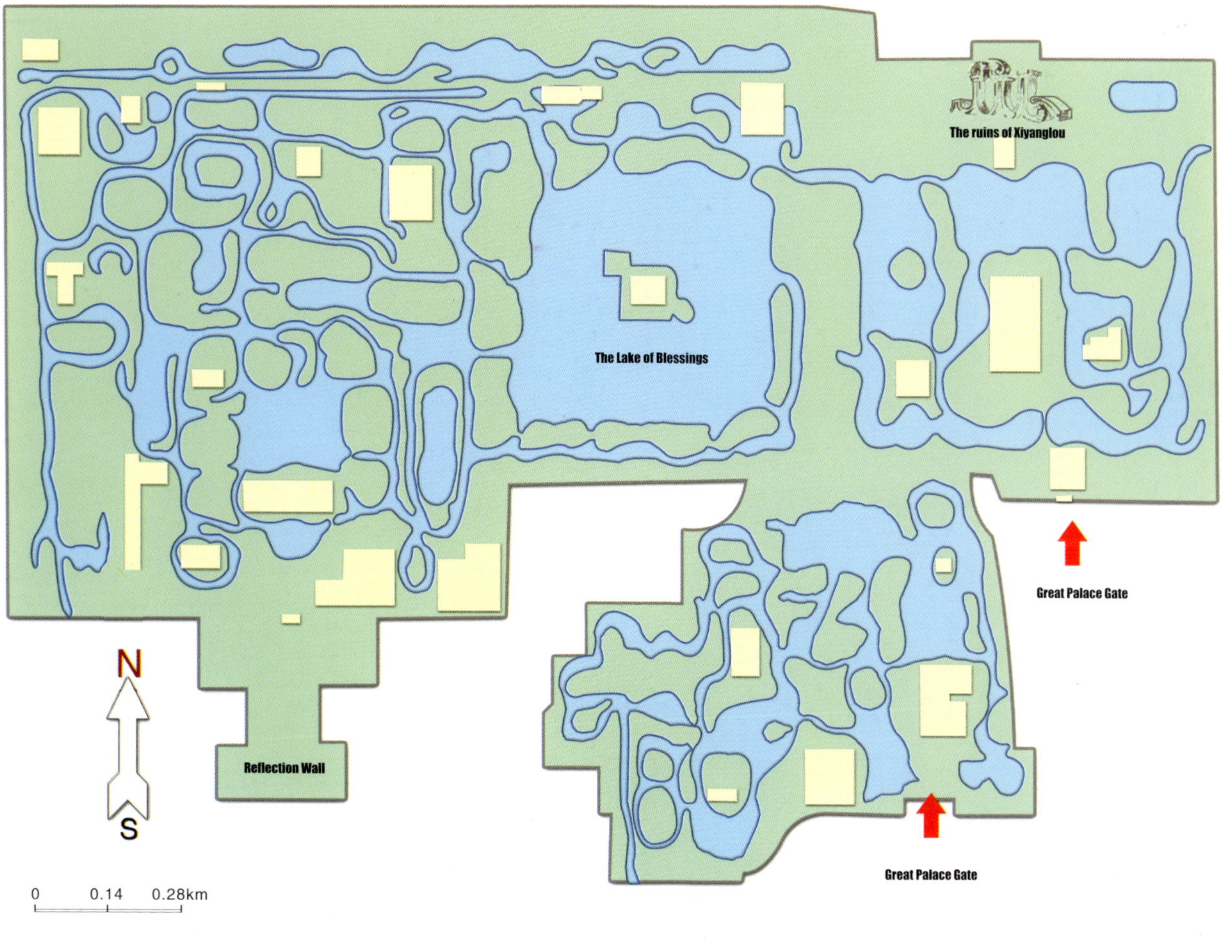

1 A bird's eye view of Fragrant Hill

2 Though this picture is far from beautiful, yet it provides us with important knowledge the ecosystem to be found at Fragrant Hill consisting of trees, bushes and grasse is quite representative of Beijing's ecosystem.

3 Spectacles Lake: man-made, but in harmony with nature.

3. Fragrant Hills

Fragrant Hills Park lies in the west of Haidian District, 20 kilometers from the city centre, and 5 kilometers west of the Summer Palace. Its location in Beijing is similar to Fontainebleau in Paris. Fragrant Hill is a mountainside imperial garden, corresponding to Corcovado Mountain in Rio de Janeiro of Brazil. From the top of Fragrant Hills, you have an excellent overall view of Beijing.

The highest peak of the Fragrant Hills chain is Xianglufeng, 557 meters high, a little lower than Corcovado Mountain (704 meters). There's a summer resort here. Here on the hill are temples and Chinese villas. Similar to Corcovado Mountain in Rio de Janeiro, there are western-style villas at the west foot of Fragrant Hill. It takes about 50 minutes to climb to the peak, and is the favor of mountain-climbers. With lakes and hills, Jingyi Garden, one of the most famous four gardens of Qing Dynasty stands at the south foot of Fragrant Hills. Just inside the north gate of the park sits the famous Spectacles Lake. The lake actually consists of two ponds linked by a stone bridge. The twin lakes resemble a pair of spectacles, hence comes the name. Fragrant Hill's Cherry Valley is also a famous water-rich area. However, over the past century, following the rapid expansion and development of the city, commercial as well as home water use has markedly increased. With the resulting decrease in ground water, Cherry Valley's water reserves have shrunk notably. You've probably seen similar phenomena in your own home region.

If you want to have a knowledge about the history of Beijing's ecosystem, you must make a trip to Fragrant Hills,

as it is a natural ecological museum of Beijing. People argued about whether there should be more trees or there should be more grass. The true meaning of a "green Olympics" is to keep harmonious with nature, namely to recover the ecosystem. Fragrant Hill is an ecosystem made up of a 300-year-old secondary forest in the suburbs of Beijing. Here you can see arbor wood, crossbar and herbaceous varieties growing in a semi-humid environment. However, due to deforestation connected with the huge construction projects of the early 1400s, much of the original virgin forest was lost. Even to this day the forest has not completely recovered. In the past century, what changes have occurred in your home area? These examples speak clearly: humankind, even if given several hundred years' time, would find it difficult to repay its debt to the world's ecosystem. Our world should be one progressing steadily toward wealth and plenty; our dream should be the harmonious development of both man and nature.

Beside the vegetation and water-rich areas of Fragrant Hills Park, there are cultural heritages as well. Built in 1331, the famous Biyun Temple is located at the east foot of the hill. When Mr. Sun Zhongshan (1866-1925), who founded the Republic of China, passed away in 1925, his coffin had temporarily placed here in Biyun Temple. Wofo Temple was built in the middle of the 7th century. Here can be found a copper sleeping Buddha of 5 meters in length, hence the name. Halfway to Xianglu Peak, is Xiangwuku—an imperial villa on the hill. Built in 1745, but burned by French and British troops in 1860. The villa was restored in 2003.

Fragrant Hills is also home to a small but worth-seeing museum. It is here that the Chinese Shakespeare—the author of *Dream of the Red Chamber*, Cao Xueqin (1715-1763 or 1764) once lived. In 2006 the teleplay of Dream of the Red Chamber recruited the actors. Surprisingly, more than 300 thousand people took part in the recruitment examination, which has created a record in the country, and could accounted for the tremendous impact of this work. Different from Shakespeare, Cao was from a rich and powerful family. Later the family fell into tough times. As a result, they moved from city to outskirts in the 1750s. Here on the wall you can see poems written by Cao's friends. My father, Dr Wu Enyu, was a doctoral student of Professor H.J. Laski, a famous professor of the London School of Economics and Political Science and an authority of the theory of International Socialism. He was also schoolmate of the former American president John F. Kennedy, and a professor at Peking University. The former Canadian Prime Minister Pienre Elliott Trudeau and the former Australian Prime Minister Gough Whitlam were also Professor H.J. Laski's students, and at present are still living. My father fully understood the value of these cultural relics, and took part in the establishment of this small but famous museum. Now that you know this, when you come to China, why don't you take the time to visit this museum? We are all from the same world, and it's a small one after all.

Similar to Da Vinci's *Mona Lisa*, which broke the artistic mould of "a thousand subjects, one face", *Dream of the Red Chamber* broke the tradition of the Chinese fiction —"a thousand books, the same story". It is the dividing line in Chinese literature history. Also, just like the study of Shakespeare in Britain or the study of Sholokhov in Russia, the debate over Cao Xueqin's works is quite lively.

4 The living conditions of Cao's later years may be the worst of the world's great authors, of example cannot be compared to those of Shakespeare; however, Cao wrote the masterpiece *Dream of the Red Chamber.*

5 This inscription on the wall of Cao's house is the evidence that this was his residence. Though grand architecture may crumble with the centuries, a written masterpiece will live on with humanity.

The Badaling Great Wall

4. The Great Wall

According to a Greek legend, the Great Wall of China was part of the Seven Wonders of the World. But such wonders as the Hanging Gardens of Babylon and Lighthouse of Alexandria have long since disappeared. Later on, the list was shortened to four: the Great Wall of China (Construction began in 214 B.C., and finished in the 16th century. The overall length is 6,300 kilometers, 629 kilometers of which are in the Beijing region); Angkor Wat of Cambodia (built from 802 to 1201); the Taj Mahal of India (built from 1631 to1653), and Borobudur of Indonesia (built about 817- 832). I have personally visited these four great monuments of human achievement. Each one is a marvelous cultural heritage, having its own breathtaking features. But when I think of the length of time spent in its construction, its sheer size and complexity, as well as the great difficulty of the project, I must say that the Great Wall impresses me the most. The Great Wall has been listed in the World Intangible and Cultural Heritage.

The Badaling Great Wall sits atop craggy mountain ranges. When you see this huge engineering project of 2000 years ago; when you think of the Pyramids of Egypt, ask yourself, "What kind of 'Pyramids' and 'Great Walls' should today's people be building?" I think to restore the eco-system is our unavoidable task.

1 A view of the Great Wall from a watchtower.

2 Badaling is the north gate of Beijing.

3 Having been to the Great Wall, you are a real man.

4 As the function of the Great Wall is for military defense, these emplacements are indispensable.

5 Not until modern times could we have a splendid night at the Great Wall. In the past, there was nothing but cold wind and inky blackness. The conditions faced by the Great Wall guard were far worse than those of the 19th century cowboys in the Rocky Mountains of America.

If you think the Great Wall was merely a mighty engineering feat, then you are mistaken. When looking out over the endless chain of mountains to the north of the Great Wall you can experience indescribable—this kind of feeling can only be rivaled by climbing to the top of such television towers as that in Canberra of Australia or the one in Brasilia, Brazil. Standing on the Great Wall, you can feel just how short life is in the long flow of history. Besides, you can also feel the greatness of the earth, and your own smallness.

However, a wonder that most travelers fail to realize is the miracle of engineering and organization that the Great Wall represents. While working on solving Beijing's water resource problem, I have been run about all over the mountains to the north of Beijing. I think to carry out such a huge project in treacherous mountains such as these must have required a chief engineer. At that time there were no maps and remote sensors. How did the builders ensure that the segments of Great Wall would exactly connect without leaving abandoned sections to later generations? It is really a miracle—even a mystery—of architectural programming and construction. So then, when we are praising great exploits of the workers and Emperor Chin Shihhuang, we should not forget the contributions made by intellectuals, especially the engineers. This knowledge can help promote visitors understanding of the Great Wall.

It took 18 centuries to build the Great Wall—from 214 B.C. to the late 16th century. It starts in the west from Jiayu Valley, near the great desert of Xinjiang in northwest China, and traverses all the way to Shanhaiguan along the Bohai Sea of Heibei Province on China's eastern seaboard. The Great Wall that we see today to the north of Beijing was mainly built in the early Ming Dynasty (latter half of the 15th century), Apart from these sections, there is another approximately 2,500 kilometers of Great Wall, built during the 16 centuries preceding the Ming Dynasty, winding through Gansu, Inner Mongolia, Shanxi, Heibei and ending up north of Beijing.

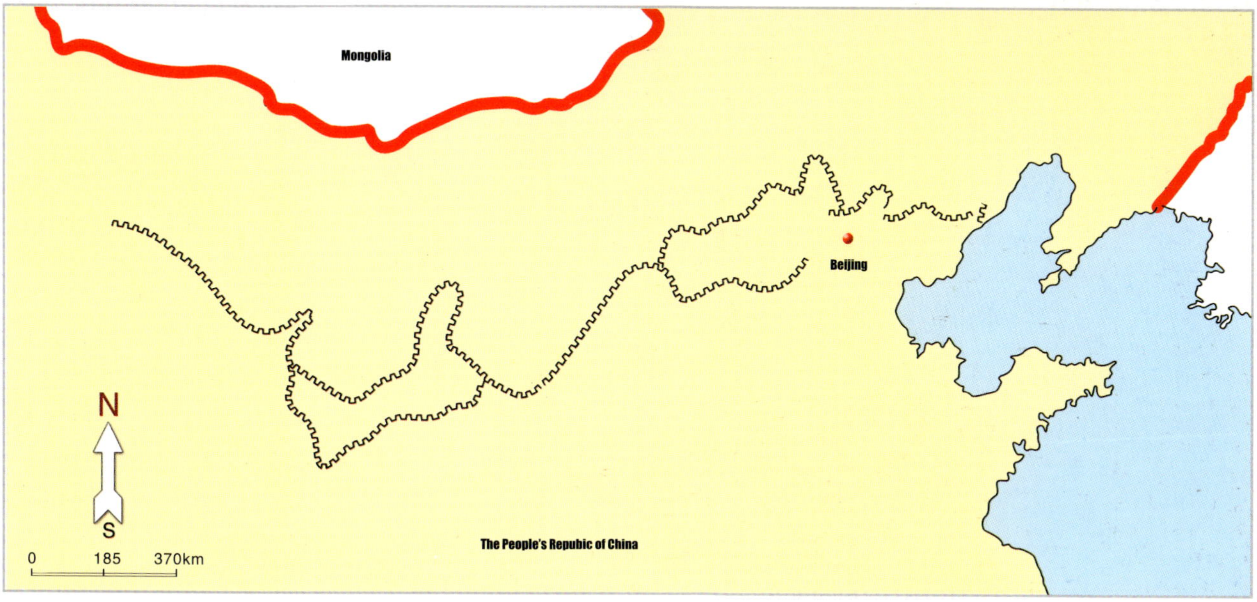

The Great Wall across the provinces

5. The Ming Tombs

In the outskirts of Beijing lies an imperial mausoleum of gigantic proportions. It is this mausoleum that makes Beijing similar to Cairo, and at the same time distinguishes these two from the rest of the world's capital cities. Of course, the Ming Tombs were built 4,000 years after those in Cairo of Egypt. The Pyramids were built above ground, while the mausoleum in Beijing is underground. The Ming Tombs are located in Changping District, about 44 kilometers to the north of Beijing. Construction started in 1409 and did not end until 1644, the fall of the Ming Dynasty. There are a total of 13 tombs. The mausoleum is on the World Heritage List. The road leading to the tombs is known as shendao, meaning "the way of the spirit". The road is line with 24 stone statues of lions, horses, elephants, camels and kylins as well as 12 stone carvings of officers and soldiers. The stone work dates back to the year 1435.

1 The Ming Tombs
2 Changling – the tomb of Emperor Zhu Di.
3 Wolong pine tree.
4 The largest pear tree in Beijing can be found at Changling. It is also known as the Guilong Tree.
5 Shendao lead the emperor to heaven.
6 The Jingang Wall of Dingling is as thick as 4 meters, one of the thickest walls in the world.
7 Coffins of the Emperor and his two wives.

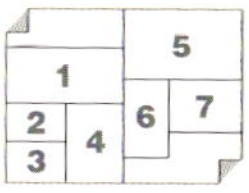

One of the tombs now open to pubic is Changling. It is the tomb of Emperor Zhu Di (reigned 1403-1424) who built up Beijing and sent minister Zheng He sailing across the seas (Zheng He left China in 1405, half a century earlier than Columbus, reaching as far as modern-day Tanzania on the African coast. His explorations ended in 1433; there were no more maritime expeditions in later dynasties). Changling was built in 1413.

Ming Tower of Dingling

Dingling is the tomb of the 13th Ming Emperor Wanli (Zhu Yijun, reigned 1573-1620) finished in 1593. The underground palace covers an area of 1,195 square meters. Its white marble gate is 3.3 meters high and 1.8 meters wide, weighing 4 tons. The roof of this underground chamber lies buried some 27 meters beneath the earth. The under ground wall—called Jingang Wall—was constructed using 56 layers of brick. Emperor Wanli and his two wives' coffins lie here within the tomb.

There are 11 tombs still to be excavated. There has been argument as to whether or not excavation is necessary. As far as I am concerned, it is still necessary, but in the process of excavation, special care must be taken in the protection of cultural relics. I hope that the next time you visit Beijing you will be able to admire even more of the Ming Tombs.

Yongling awaiting excavation

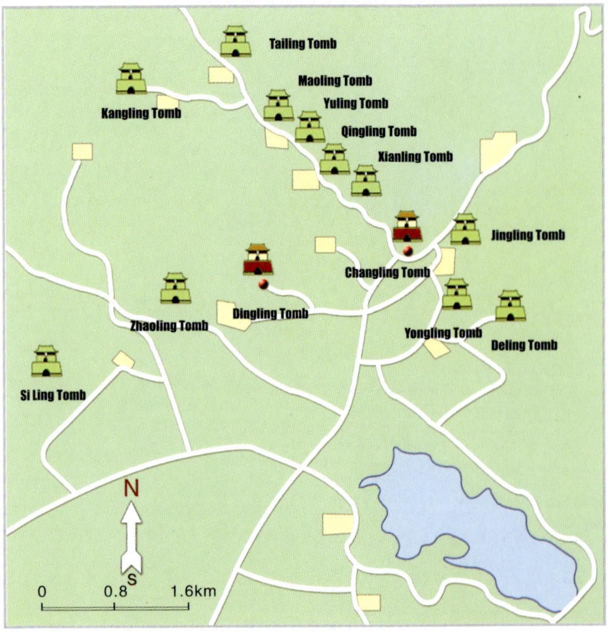

Beijing's Olympic Park under construction. The " Water Cube" on the left top is a modern stadium.

China's adorable national treasure, the Giant Panda

The western style front gate of the Beijing Zoo was built in 1906 at the end of the Qing Dynasty. At that time it was the Sanbeizi Garden of the imperial family.

6. The Olympic Park

Beijing's parks are not all ancient; there are modern ones as well. In preparation for the Olympics, the Beijing Olympic Park is under construction. It is about 7 kilometers due north of the Forbidden City, covering 1215 hectares (including an Olympic Forest Park of 760 hectares). This is indeed the largest park in Beijing, exceeding the Versailles park in Paris. Not only the main stadiums, the Olympic Village, Media Centre and National folk Museum, but also a broad area of "green land "and forest are located in this region.

There are still many other parks in Beijing, such as the Beijing Zoo on Xizhimenwai Street in Xicheng District. Built in 1908, it is one of the famous parks in the world. There are about 6,000 animals of about 600 different kinds. In 1982, the famous Thoiry safari park 40 kilometers west of Paris presented the Beijing Zoo two precious hybridized animals—a couple of lion-tigers, who lived in the Beijing Zoo for 14 years. They have been an oft-repeated story of Sino-French friendship.

Religion and Confucianism in Beijing

Even though China doesn't have a leading religion, it is home to the world's main religions. The city of Beijing displays the cultural diversity of these religions. Our world includes myriads of cultures, and our dream is to realize their harmonious cooperation.

Confucian Temple

Yonghegong Lamasery (Lama Temple)

White Cloud Taoist Temple (Baiyunguan)

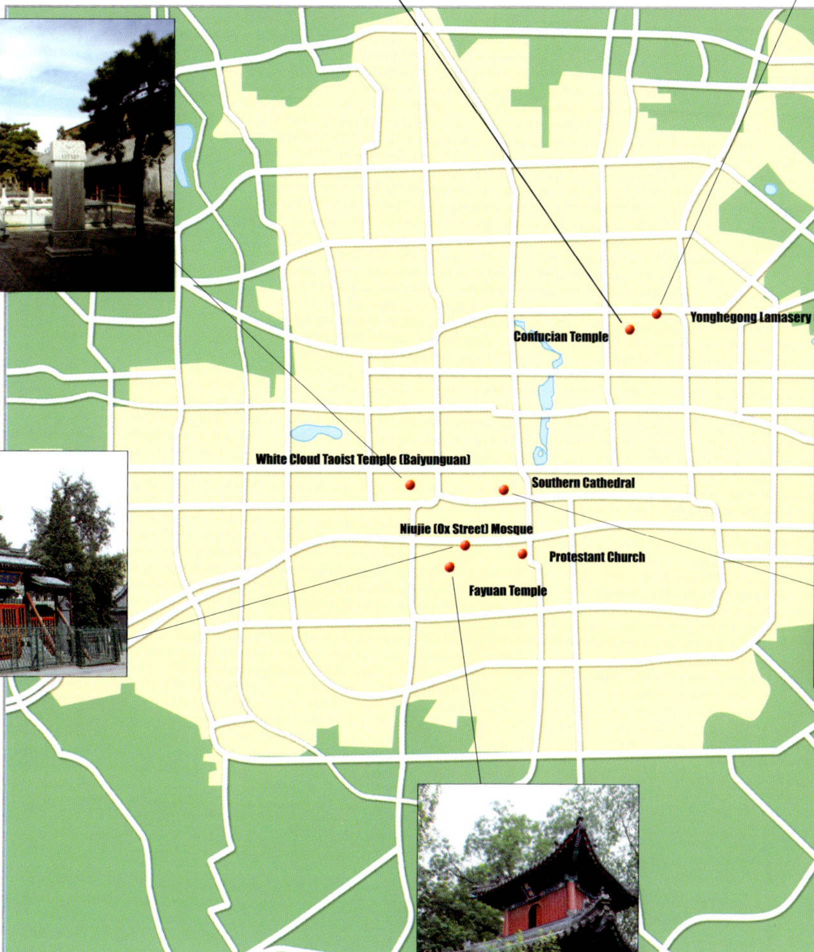

Niujie (Ox Street) Mosque

Southern Cathedral

Fayuan Temple

0 2.3 4.6km

Fayuan Temple, the most ancient temple in Beijing

The Drum Tower of Fayuan Temple. Drum towers are an absolute necessity to Beijing's temples.

1. Buddhism

Buddhism had been the primary religion of China several times since it first entered from India in the 2nd century B.C. In the 6th century, China became the centre for the spread of Buddhism.

In 645 A.D., Fayuan Temple was set up in Beijing's Xuanwu District. At one point it served as the Jin Dynasty civil service examination site. Today it is the Chinese Buddhist Academy. Like the Saint German Church, the oldest building in Paris, Fayuan Temple is Beijing's oldest extant temple.

Wanfuge of Yonghegong Lamasery

Day in and day out, Buddhist pilgrims stream into Yonghegong Lamasery

This sandalwood statue in Wanfuge is the biggest such statue in the world.

Just as Christianity is divided into Catholicism, the Orthodox Church and Protestantism, Buddhism has different branches in China. Lamaism, which evolved in Tibet and prevails in the regions of Tibet and Inner Mongolia, is a very important branch. Located in the north-east part of Beijing's Dongcheng District, Yonghegong Lamasery (Lama Temple) was built in 1694 as the former Qing Dynastic building and was converted into a lamasery in 1744. Wanfuge (Ten-Thousand-Happiness Pavilion) ,majestic and magnificent, is the main building of the Lama Temple. Of interest to visitors is Wanfuge's 18-metre high sandalwood statue. It was engraved from a 26-metre long white sandalwood log in 1753, and is the biggest stand-up wooden statue in the world. Day in and day out , Buddhist pilgrims stream into the temple.

The "martial general" of Tianwangdian

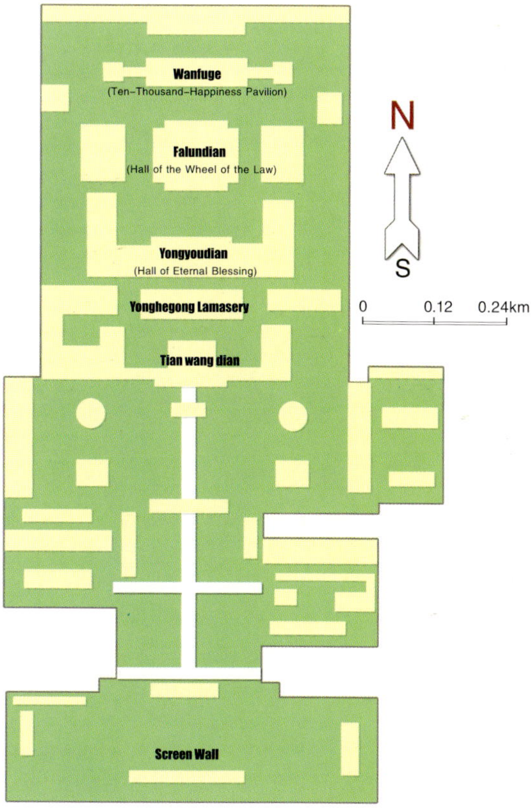

Kwan-yin, the goddess of Buddhism.

2. Taoism

Taoism originated in mainland China in the 1st century A.D. It is said that Taoism originated with the thoughts of legendary Chinese Emperor Huang as well as the famous Chinese philosopher Laozi (who is thought to have lived during the 6th-5th century B.C.). At one point, Taoism also became the primary religion of China. Built in 739 A.D., situated near Guang'anmen of Beijing's Xuanwu District, Baiyunguan (White Cloud Taoist Temple) is the largest one of its kind. The existing structure was rebuilt during the Qing Dynasty.

The gate of White Cloud Taoist Temple (Baiyunguan)

White Cloud Taoist Temple (Baiyunguan) is the most representative of Chinese style temples.

1 Confucian Temple, Imperial College.

2 A famous structure inside the Confucian Temple.

3 One of the monuments donated by emperors and other notable figures throughout the dynasties, located here in the Confucian temple.

4 A statue of Kongzi

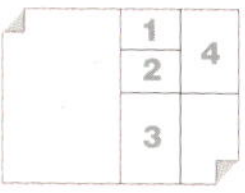

3. Confucianism

Though Confucian Thought—the thoughts of Kongzi (551 B.C.-479 B.C.) — is not a kind of religion, yet its effect in molding the beliefs and regulating the morals of the Chinese people, was much greater than any religion. Because of this, many foreign scholars believe that Confucian Thought is basically the same as a religion. The Confucian Temple on Imperial College Street of Dongcheng District was set up in 1302. It is a place in which sacrifices are offered to Kongzi. The modern Chinese concepts of a " harmonious society" and a " harmonious world" are actually the continuation and further development of certain Confucian ideas.

4. Islam

Islam was spread to China in 757 A.D. In the year 996 A. D., a mosque was built on Xuanwu District's Niujie (Ox Street). This mosque was rebuilt time and time again over the years. The Mosque continues the style of traditional Chinese temples, but its decorations are in after the traditional Islamic style. Later on, Niujie (Ox Street) became a Muslim neighborhood. Near the mosque is the China Islamic Association.

Niujie (Ox Street) Mosque

China Islamic Association

5. Christianity

Christianity entered China as early as 635 A.D., and was approved by the first emperor of Tang Dynasty, Tang Taizong (reigned 627-649). The Italian missionary Matteo Ricci (1552-1610) set up a cathedral on Xuanwu District's West Qianmen Street in the early 17th century. In 1650, German missionary Johann Adam Schall von Bell (1591-1666) set up a Protestant church known as the Southern Cathedral. The existing building was rebuilt as a Catholic Church in 1904. At present, Beijing has four Christian churches. European missionaries brought European law, painting, science and technology to China as they evangelized. Their work had a great effect on the development of Chinese modern science. Emperor Kangxi of the Qing Dynasty (reigned1661-1722) learned geometry from missionaries such as Johann Adam Schallvon Bell, and others.

The new church in Guang'an Street, Xuanwu District is built after the Elizabethan style.

Inside the Southern Cathedral on Qianmen West Street, Xuanwu District.

The Southern Cathedral at Qianmen is European neo-classical architecture.

" First there was the Pool and Cudrania Temple, then came Beijing."

6. Buddhist Temples in the Suburbs of Beijing

In contrast with Japan's Buddhist temples, most of which are built in cities, China has a considerable number of temples established in the mountains, some of these being built deep in the wilderness in order to isolate the devout from the outside world. There are many Buddhist temples in the suburbs of Beijing such as the famous Pool and Cudrania Temples as well as Jietaisi (Ordination Terrace Temple) in Mentougou District.

On the side of Tanzhe Mountain stands the Pool and Cudrania Temple, which is situated 40 kilometers from the centre of Beijing. It was set up in the 5th century A.D. and got its name from its Dragon Pool and the cudrania trees on the hill behind the temple. For centuries there has been a saying: " First there was the Pool and Cudrania Temple, and then came Beijing." So the pattern of inner Beijing is similar to that of the Pool and Cudrania Temple. The temple contains the tomb of Buddhist Miaoyan, the daughter of the Yuan Dynasty's first emperor, Kublai Khan. Inside the temple, there is the magnificient Mahavira Hall (Daxiongbaodian). In the courtyard trees, several hundred years old, stretch for the skies.

Located on the mountainside of Ma'anshan (Saddle Hill) in Mentougou District, Jietaisi (Ordination Terrace Temple) lies 35 kilometers southwest of the city centre and about 10 kilometers southeast of the Pool and Cudrania Temple. The temple was set up in 622 A.D. The existing building was built during the Qing Dynasty, and contains a three-story Ordination Altar(3.5 meters in height, made of white marble). In the courtyard there are ancient pines of all different shapes and sizes, some of which are over 1,000 years.

Inside of the Pool and Cudrania Temple

Ordination Terrace Temple is well-known for its many ancient pines.

Beijing is the cultural centre of China and also a flourishing city of culture, education, science and technology.

1.Education of Beijing

Tsinghua University, Peking University and Beijing University of Aeronautics and Astronautics are well known around the world. These universities have some of the world's most outstanding and talented students, some of whom become part of China's leadership, and some become world renowned scholars. Since I received an outstanding education in Beijing, I can testify to the high quality of the educational system here.

Many noted figures of recent Chinese history had strolled along the Weiming Lake of Peking University.

Honglou, the original main building of Peking University, was the launch pad of the May Fourth Movement – the movement that started China on the road to a brighter future.

As a child, I lived in the dormitory of the original Peking University and grew up under the influence of Honglou ("Red Building", literally). Originally located in the midwest part of Dongcheng District, Peking University was founded in 1908. Honglou is the symbol of Peking University, just as the Sorbonne Church symbolizes Parisian University. The difference is that Honglou was set up in 1909, while the Sorbonne Church was completed in 1642. Peking University moved to its new home in 1952, where it stands to this day. It is located near the Summer Palace in Haidian District and on the ruins of Yanyuan and Changchunyuan (Garden of Everlasting Spring) which were Beijing's notable parks in the Qing Dynasty, but were destroyed by Anglo-French allied forces in 1860. Beautiful Weimin Lake has become the symbol of today's Peking University.

Beichizi Primary School
(formerly Ninghe Temple)

The rebuilt gate of the Second Middle School of Beijing

In 1950, I entered Beichizi Primary School, a well known school in Dongcheng District. The school was Ninghe Temple before. Just as many of India's Buddhist temples are also schools and many European churches were also educational centers, most of the primary schools in Beijing at that time were temples.

In 1956, I entered the No.2 Middle School of Beijing in Dongcheng District. It was also a well known school with a long history. The school was originally set up in 1724 as a Manchu military school, and became a modern high school in 1910.

The only remnant of the old Qinghuayuan (today's Tsinghua University) is this Memorial Archway, now known as Tsinghua University's Second gate. Many noted political and economic figures have passed by this gate.

Water scenery near the " Waste Islands", which during the Qing Dynasty was known as Jinchunyuan.

The gate of Beihang University (Beijing University of Aeronautics and Astronautics). The university has cultivated much Chinese astronautic talent.

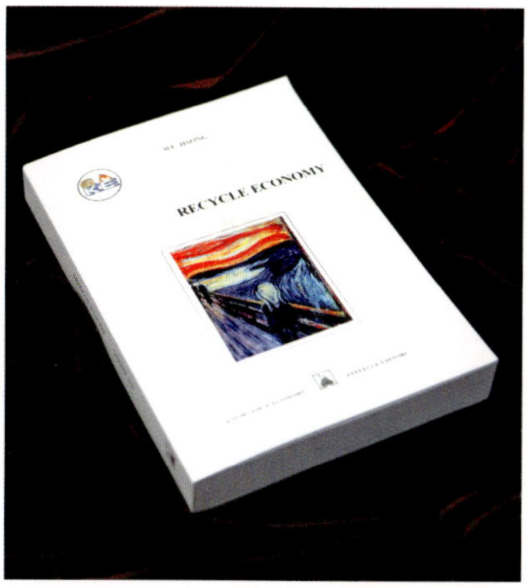

English Version of *New Recycle Economics* by Prof. Wu Jisong, published by Italian Effeelle Press in 2006

In 1962 I enrolled in the well-known Tsinghua University, founded in 1911. Tsinghuayuan was also a part of the ruins of Imperial Gardens destroyed by Anglo-French allied forces in 1860 and has one of the most beautiful university campuses in Beijing today.

Beihang University (Beijing University of Aeronautics and Astronautics) is a fairly new university, built in 1952. It is one of the most well known universities in Beijing, as well as in all of China. I am currently the Dean of the Economics & Management school at Beihang. From my office, you can see the office building belonging to the Beijing Olympic Games Organizing Committee, off in the distance. Social science research is quite advanced here in Beijing. At present the whole world is studying the factors contributing to China's booming and successful economic growth, researches done by the Chinese are naturally the most note-worthy. For example, the China Centre for Recycle Economy Research, based at Beihang University. Its research on Knowledge Economy and Recycle Economy currently leads the world.

A corner of the Economics & Management School building of Beihang University. As one of the largest main buildings of Chinese Universities, the sprawling complex covers 227,000 square meters, which is 1.5 times the size of the Forbidden City.

Beijing is currently working hard to produce more and more international talent characterized by modern thinking and high personal culture. When you visit Beijing's universities, you will see in your mind's eye Beijing's future.

2.Science & Technology and Environment of Beijing

Beijing takes knowledge economy as its development direction. It not only occupies a leading role in many scientific research projects but also emphasizes the significance of industrialization. At present, it has already become a booming, developing city of high-tech industry. The annual economic growth rate of Beijing has exceeded 10 percent for the last 8 years. Beijing's per capita GDP exceeded 6,000 dollars in 2006. Zhongguancun is the centre of Beijing's scientific research, at the heart of which lie the Research Institutes of the Chinese Academy of Sciences, Peking University and Tsinghua University, gathering an army of some 500,000 researchers—more than America's Silicon Valley. Looking at it today, no one could imagine that 100 years ago, this very spot was the burial ground for eunuchs of the Qing Dynasty, and that even fifty years ago, their graves could still be seen. What a change has occurred during the last 50 years! The Beijing Experimental Zone for the Development of New Technological Industries was set up on the base of Zhongguancun Science & Technology Development Park in the early 1980s. The centre of this zone lies to the south of Tsinghua University, Haidian District, with 17,000 high-tech companies occupying an area of 232,000 square meters with more than 626,000 employees. These companies produced a GDP of 12 billion dollars in 2005 which occupy 14 percent of Beijing' GDP. The exports of these companies accounted for nearly 20 percent of that of Beijing in 2005. 148 of the world's top enterprises have branches here, including 65 research institutions. Zhongguancun's industry is entering the world stage through "new industrialization".

Beijing Olympic Games building

Beijing Experimental Zone for the Development of New Technological Industries

Beijing is protecting and repairing the ecosystem, believing that man and nature should be in harmony. From the late 20th Century, the increase of Beijing's population, the development of production and the improvement of the standard of living, have put great pressure on the environment. Plus with years of drought during the last part of the 20th Century, Beijing is short of water. After approval by the State Council, The Capital City Sustainable Water Resources Program was put into effect in 2001. At the same time, before the 2008 Olympic, Beijing's sewage disposal rate will exceed 60 percent, while the recycled water rate will reach 65 percent. The program will not only ensured the water supply of Beijing and a "green Olympics", but will also restore the water ecosystem of Beijing. A piece of noteworthy information: The steel-making factory, Capital Steel Corporation has been moved from Beijing to Hebei Province as of 2006. The factory will be rebuilt according to the principles of recycle economics and clean production. Taking this action alone will cut Beijing's air pollution by almost a third. Furthermore, Beijing has taken great strides in the areas of reducing the production of the so-called " single-use" products, classifying garbage and the safe disposal of solid waste.

Led by advanced technology, Beijing should implement recycle economy, repair its ecosystem and build a harmonious international metropolis—one with the ability to make a sustainable development. Beijing should build a city with developed production, a balanced ecosystem, and most of all, with good living conditions.

Chuangye Mansion, the incubator of Zhongguancun

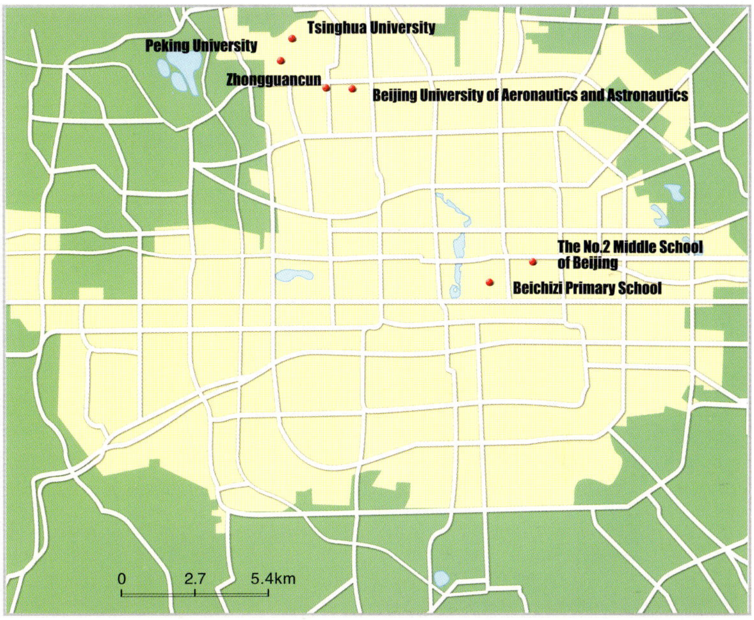

Restoring the water system of Beijing

Foods and Business of Beijing

A frequently told joke at the United Nations Educational, Scientific and Cultural Organization (UNESCO) during the time that I worked there was that: the happiest person in the world is one "earning U.N. (United Nations) wages, living in Paris and enjoying Chinese food" . China's food culture not only has a long history, but is also well known around the world.

1. Foods of Beijing

As the centre of Chinese culture, Beijing's food culture is flourishing. Here in Beijing you can enjoy delicious food from all over the world. There are four types of Chinese cuisine: Lu (Shandong), Su (Jiangsu and Zhejiang), Chuan (Sichuan) and Yue (Guangdong).

Beijing cuisine has its own special unique features. Beijing Roast Duck has gained an international reputation. The oldest restaurant offering roast duck is Quanjude ,which means "repository of all virtues". Its original version was set up in 1864 on Qianmen Street in Xuanwu District. Now it has a number of branches. Their duck-roasting methods have already attained the level of art. Watching the slicing of roast duck has turned into a kind of "art appreciation". At Quanjude, while enjoying roast duck, you can also taste delicious delicacies from the four major Chinese food styles.

Roasting Ducks

Roast ducks

Slicing the roast duck onto the platter

Quanjude Roast Duck Restaurant

Roast duck—or often referred to as Peking Duck—is a feature dish of Beijing, originated in the army of Genghis Khan in the Yuan Dynasty.

Another well-known style of food is Imperial Cuisine, among which Manhanquanxi in Fangshan Restaurant of Beihai Park is a famous one. Fangshan Restaurant was opened in 1925 by a previous royal chief.

Fangshan Restaurant, located in Beihai Park, provides lake-front imperial cuisine with a view of a tower in the distance.

Manhanquanxi Hall is as magnificent as the famous Nation Restaurant in Moscow.

Tan Cuisine is not only fine food but also a form of art. Since it is art, it is hard to say which is good and which is bad. You must decide for yourself which you like and which you dislike?

Tan Cuisine Hall in the ancient Beijing Hotel.

Tan cuisine originated in the household of Tan Zongjun, a minister in the Qing Dynasty, and is now offered at the Beijing Hotel, built in 1906. Yue—or better known as Cantonese— style food and Huaiyang style dishes are also well known in the Beijing Hotel.

The "Hot Pot" on the table is the special cooking ware for boiled mutton.

In the dark, Donglaisun Restaurant reminds one of the famous Mongolian conqueror, Genghis Khan. I'm sure that Genghis Khan would never have imagined that the food used to allay his soldier's hunger would one day became famous Beijing cuisine.

The Donglaisun Restaurant, which was built in Wangfujing Street in 1903, offers Mutton Hot Pot.

There are also famous restaurants of Lu, Chuang and Huaiyang style dishes. Fengzeyuan Restaurant on Zhushikou Street in Xuanwu District was built in 1930 and serves Lu style dishes.

The original Sichuan Restaurant was rebuilt by the Royal Restaurant and renamed by the former Prime Minister Zhou Enlai (1898-1976) in 1959. The restaurant is now located in Prince Gong's Garden in Liuying Street by Shicha Lake in Xicheng District.

Fengzeyuan Restaurant was built in 1930.

This Sichuan Restaurant deals in Chuan style dishes.

The staple food of Lu style dishes is Chinese style bread-all kinds of Mantou.

The special atmosphere of an evening garden banquet.

1 Jiumen Snack Town at Shicha Lake

2 All kinds of snacks

3 Tea soup, Chinese Coca Cola

The other representative of Beijing's food culture is its snacks. You can taste an assortment of numerous different snacks at the traditional Jiumen Snack Town of Shicha Lake in Dongcheng District. This snack town is somewhat similar to the chophouses along the La Seine in Paris. Tea soup (Chatang) is a unique Beijing beverage.

Staving traveled to 80 countries, I have realized that no matter how picky you are about food, you will want to eat your home country's food at least once a week when abroad. I can assure you, Beijing can satisfy you completely. I am very surprised by the fact that Chinese people seem to be accepting foreign food at a much faster rate than that at which foreigners are accepting Chinese food.

You can taste French food at the Peace Hotel of Dongcheng District.

Peace Hotel lies to the north of Wangfujing Street, the most flourishing place in Beijing.

Is the interior of Peace Hotel Marseilles style?

The Brazil Grilled Meat Store is surrounded by Beijing's typical folk house, Siheyuan, near Xidan, at the center of the city.

Inside the Brazil Grilled Meat Store

For South American food, go to the Brazil Grilled Meat Store of Xicheng District.

You can enjoy Japanese food at the Beijing New Otani Chang Fu Gong Hotel of Chongwen District and you don't have to sit on the ground.

Outside of Beijing's New Otani Chang Fu Gong Hotel

Inside of Beijing's New Otani Chang Fu Gong Hotel. Outside the window is a Japanese-style garden.

Moscow Restaurant, from the inside

A view of Sanlitun's Bar Street

For a taste of Russian food, go to the Moscow Restaurant with 50 years history located in Haidian District.

There is also the well known Sanlitun Bar Street in Chaoyang District. It is a popular place for young people, with cafes packed in more densely than at Boulevard St. German Street of Paris.

Outside the Great Wall Sheraton Hotel.

Inside the Great Wall Sheraton Hotel.

You can taste American food at The Great Wall Sheraton Hotel of Chaoyang District. And there have been about 90 shops of McDonald's and 160 shops of KFC (Kentucky Fried Chicken) in Beijing since the first snack bar set up in 1978. The biggest innovation of American-style short order is that a restaurant will not rely on notable kitcheners but on standardization.

For German cuisine, head to the Beijing Kempinski Hotel of Chaoyang District.The German style pigs legs have a distinctive flavour.

Beijing's Kempinski Hotel, from the outside.

Kempinski Hotel, from the inside.

Fragrant Hill Hotel—a place with Chinese and western characters—is located on Fragrant Hill Street in Haidian District. The hotel was designed by a famous Chinese-American architect. Here you can enjoy any type cuisines both from China and from other countries in the whole world.

Inside Fragrant Hill Hotel.

Outside Fragrant Hill Hotel.

Fragrant Hill Hotel

The Great Wall Sheraton Hotel

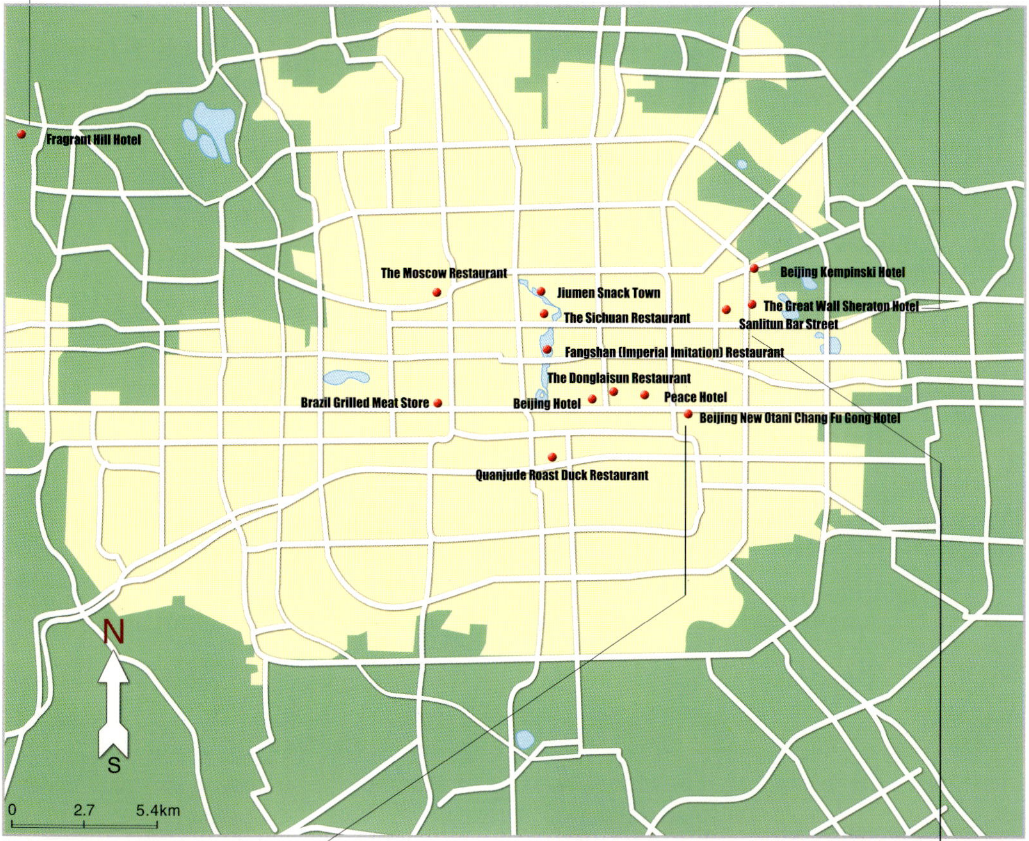

Beijing New Otani Chang Fu Gong Hotel

Sanlitun Bar street

2. Business in Beijing

Business in Beijing is developing very well. The most famous business area is Wangfujing Street just east of the Forbidden City. As with Revoli Avenue north of the Parisian Louvre Museum, Wangfujing Street was originally built for royalty. It has been converted from a traditional business street into a modern pedestrian street, which brings us a complex feeling of seeing a modernized Beijing and a sense of regret for witnessing the loss of its ancient style. Our world is changing and our dream is to realize the harmonious blending of past and future. On this street, there are not only old shops with more than one hundred years of history, but also Beijing's first general merchandise store, the Soviet-style Beijing Department Store, originally built in 1956, half a century later than the oldest department store in Paris—Au Bon Marche on Bul. St. German Avenue. The street is lined with statues suggesting Wangfujing's old days.

Wangfujing Pedestrian Street.

Wonton Hou has over one hundred years of history.

Evening market in Donghuamen – north of Wangfujing Street.

The Beijing Department Store is a typical store built after the former Soviet-style. It represents a bygone era of Beijing's history.

←Actor's statue in Wangfujing Street.

Tongshenghe, a shoe store with long history. ↑

Sellers are talking with foreign tourists in the New Silk Street Market.

Yansha Youyi Shopping City.

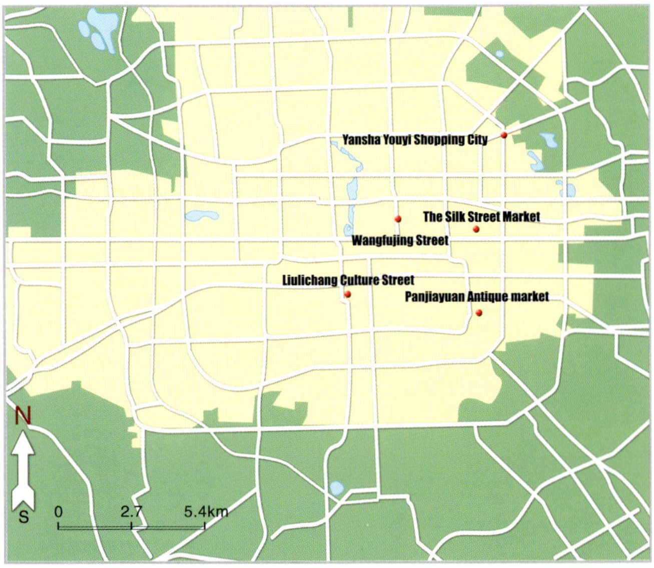

New Silk Street Market opened in 2005.

There are also quite a number of large supermarkets in Beijing from places like America, Japan, and France. Wal-Mart, Ito Yokado and Carrefour have many branches here. Apart from these three, there is the Yansha Youyi Shopping City (Beijing Lufthansa Centre), set up in 1978, which is a sino-German joint venture. The Silk Street Market is very well-known among international tourists for its fashionable clothes. Back in the 1980s, it was only a flea market, but today it becomes a fully-fledged market.

Folk Houses of Beijing

Beijing' s folk houses are unique in the world.

There are approximately four categories of folk houses to be found in the world. One kind is the chesstype represented by chang' an of the Tang Dynasty and Beijing of the Qing Dynasty (Kyoto of Japan, New York of America later copied this style); the second kind is represented by Paris, and is characterized by an expansion based on the current residential area; most cities of the world adopt this type. Another type is represented by Los Angels of America, and is characterized by the jointing of small towns with an extensive road network. The fourth type is the creation of a completely new city using man-made layout. Examples of this type are Brasilia of Brazil, Islamabad of Pakistan and Abuja of Nigeria. At present, many cities of the world carry on a combination of these four.

1. Shicha Lake Folk House Area

Located in Xicheng District, Shicha Lake Residential Area is quite typical of ancient Beijing. It sits beside clear emerald waters, with deep water-lanes cutting across it. When the 1,000-kilometer Grand Canal from Beijing to Hangzhou was opened to navigate, many people lived along the river. Shicha Lake is the end point of the Great Canal. Nowadays it is a tourist spot, complete with modern bars.

Tourists take in the view from pedicabs.

The Shicha Lake neighborhood is one of the most perfectly preserved folk house areas in Beijing.

Bars along the street at Shicha Lake.

Shicha Lake Folk House Area.

Young people in an old tea shop.

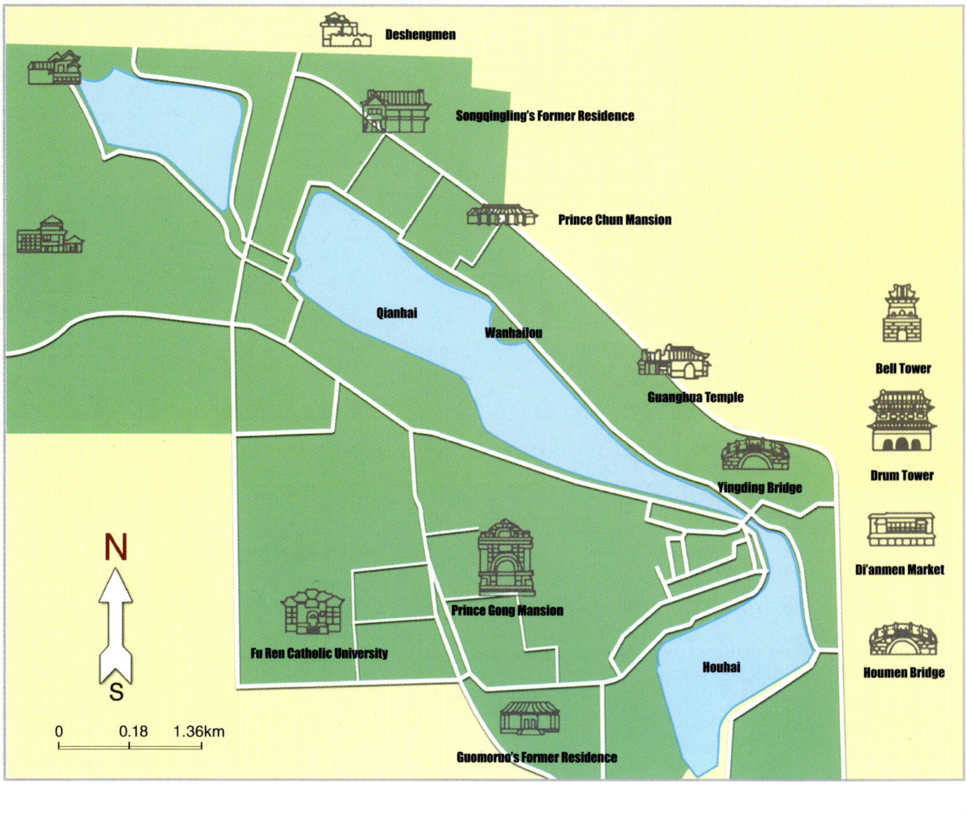

There are large trees along the perfectly preserved ancient Hutongs; Modern equipment such as air-conditioners can be seen on the wall.

Gate of a remodeled Hutong has a mixture of both Chinese and western style.

The only modern equipment visable in this small civilian Hutong is electric wire.

2. Hutongs (laneways) of Beijing

The "chess-type" old city of Beijing is made up of Hutongs (laneways). The pattern started from the 13th century(the Yuan Dynasty). In Mongolian Hutong means "well", so almost every Hutong had a well, from which you can see the abundant under-water resources that Beijing enjoyed at that time. Even now, here Beijing, there are place names such as Sanyan Well Hutong.

A foreign resident walking out of a Hutong.

3. Siheyuan (dwelling compounds) and Modern Folk Houses in Beijing

Hutongs are formed by Siheyuans lining up side-by-side on opposite sides of a street. The typical Siheyuan is a foursquare courtyard. Every courtyard has a gate; once you enter, you are met by rooms on all four sides. You can see this type of courtyard in Tokyo and Seoul now. But in general these Siheyuans only have houses on three sides of the courtyard. In reality, most of Beijing's citizens today live in modern residential areas. The residents of Beijing come from many countries; just counting Koreans, at the turn of the 21st century, Beijing had more than 100,000. The people of Beijing are warm-hearted and hospitable. In order to get ready for the Olympic Games, the residents of Siheyuans not only do their morning exercises, but also learn social manners and English in the evening.

Even though the common Siheyuan is a little crowded, the practice of designating the northwest rooms for the hosts and the southeast rooms for guests has not been changed.

The Siheyuans of the rich are spacious. They're not like storied buildings. When Beijing's residents went abroad, they had a hard time getting used to Europe's storied buildings.

There exists much debate as to what should be done with Beijing's Siheyuans—should they be saved or removed? Different from Paris, most of Beijing's Siheyuan are in poor quality and hard to preserve, so I believe it is feasible to remove some of them; at the same time I think it is also necessary to save and rebuild some. I suggest removing a third, saving a third, and remodeling a third of the Siheyuans in the old city area. In this way twin goals can be achieved—today's development and protection lf yesterday's old relics. Do you have any suggestions to make?

Purple Jade Villas of Chaoyang District, funded and built by a businessman from Taiwan Province.

The well-known East Garden in Chaoyang District.

Beijing residents doing their "morning excercises"

Doing exercises in the morning's sunshine

Playing shuttlecock in group

The Ming Tombs Reservoir, built by manpower in 1958, is 627 meters long and 29 meters high. I made my contributions to this project. The mountain forests and water-rich areas north of Beijing will soon become several tourist attractions, equal like eco-tourism region in Korea's Jeju Islands.

Satellite cities in Beijing's suburbs.

Small towns on the outskirts of Beijing.

4. Suburban Areas and Villages of Beijing

The administration area of Beijing is different from that of Paris. The suburban areas of Beijing are much larger than those of Paris. Here in Beijing, there are not only residences in the suburbs but also many small towns and villages beyond.

The farmhouses in the suburbs of Beijing mainly stick to the Siheyuan pattern. There are many small towns surrounding Beijing; some of them have developed into satellite cities. These small towns dot the countryside near the capital city, and produce fruit, vegetables and foodstuffs for Beijing.

" Snow-apples " in Beijing's suburbs

The bountiful harvest of Beijing's suburban " Fruit Garden"

The Culture of Beijing

Beijing is a city with a diversity of culture. Here is a simple introduction.

The Hu-Guang Assembly Hall Theatre was built in 1806. Audiences can drink tea while watching the opera. Compared with the Paris Theatre, which ambience is better? Perhaps it is hard to answer, which shows the diversity of the world's culture.

1. Peking Opera

The flagship of Beijing's culture—Peking Opera—came into being at the end of the 18th Century. Peking Opera is the symbol of Chinese art and has significant influence throughout the world as European Opera. Although there are no ancient Peking Opera theatres as big as the Parisian Opera House, Beijing is home to some very exquisite Chinese-style theatres with luxurious seating arrangements. The modern Chang'an Theater is a specific Peking Opera theater. In Dongcheng District, there are two famous theatres, one near Tian'anmen Square and the other on Chang'an Street. Certainly there are also many modern theaters in Beijing such as the Poly Theater in Chaoyang District and Tianqiao Theatre in Xuanwu District, etc.

The Dongyuan Theater of Changpuhe was built in 2002.

The spacious and luxurious box of Changpuhe's Dongyuan Theater.

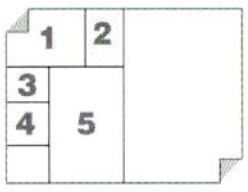

1 Performing Peking Opera

2 Peking Opera character (male)

3 The large Chang'an Theater was first built in 1937 and moved to its current location in 1996. It mainly hosts Peking Opera performances.

4 Poly Theater, built in 1984, attracts top world opera performers.

5 Peking Opera character (female)

2. Antiques

Having been the capital of four dynasties as well as a well known city with a long history, Beijing overflows with antiques. There are not only many famous antique stores on Liulichang Street in Xuanwu District, Chaoyang District's Panjiayuan Antique market is full of great selections too. Liulichang Street came into being 500 years ago during the Ming Dynasty. It is known as the No.1 Antique Street in China. Panjiayuan Market lies in the south of Chaoyang District. It was only a flea market in 1992 and has since turned into a market with world-wide recognition, serving some 60-70 thousand customers every day.

In Beijing, collecting antiques is a common practice. The hobby of collecting antiques is similar to the European-American practice of collecting paintings. There are many families in Beijing that have 200-year old antiques. From this fact you can get a feel for the depth of Beijing's culture.

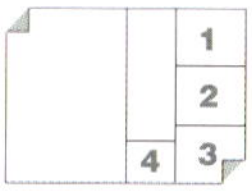

1 Liulichang Street has 500 years of history.

2 Old famous store in Liulichang street

3 Stores inside Panjiayuan Antique Market

4 The booming Panjiayuan Antique Market

3. Handicrafts

Handicrafts are another special feature of Beijing's culture. One is " face patterns" which are closely connected to Peking Opera. The patterns are of people and mythological figures from Chinese history as shown in Peking Opera. Among them is the well known monkey king Sun Wukong that can supposedly travel over 54,000 kilometers in one summersault – that's more than one trip around the earth! This was the 16th century Chinese' dream of space flight. The face pattern of "Fuwa" was the idea behind the Beijing 2008 Olympic Games mascot.

Entertainers making face patterns

The face pattern of this woman seems to have an almost Mona Lisa-like smile.

Peking Opera face patterns

The myth figure Sun Wukong

"Fuwa" face pattern

Mianren (face person) is another handicraft of Beijing. The image of the mythological character Zhongkui is quite life-like. Zhongkui was a legendary Taoist figure that resolved to remove all evil from the world. Ancient China had the custom of displaying Zhongkui's photo at home for the purpose of exorcising evil. Chinese paper-cutting is another handicraft of Beijing. Similar to the birth constellation in Europe, China has twelve animal signs, namely the Rat, Cow, Tiger, Rabbit, Dragon, Snake, Horse, Sheep, Monkey, Chicken, Dog and Pig. The paper-cut of these animals is very lively. Additional handicrafts include Chuitangren (blowing sugar) and Caobian (grass plaiting), etc.

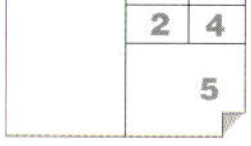

1 Making Mianren

2 Grass weaving (Cao bian)

3 Blowing sugar (chui tang ren)

4 Paper-cutting

5 Chinese Paper-cut – the twelve animal signs. The Chinese characters wish good luck and happiness to those born each year of the twelve year cycle.

The lifelike Mianren Zhongkui

4. Painting and Calligraphy

Chinese painting and calligraphy are famous all over the world. Beijing is a collecting place for these two types of traditional Chinese art. Many museums in Beijing have abundant displays of them, the most representative being that of the Palace Museum (the Forbidden City). Chinese Claborate-style painting is unique in the world; later it would have a great influence on Japanese and Korean painting. Many noted western artists believe that the Chinese painting style known as Xieyi is the prototype of the abstract painting style.

Chinese Gongbi style painting, *Qingmingshanghetu* (part)

What are the similarities and differences between Chinese Xieyi painting and western modern abstract painting?

The writing of Chinese characters is not only a kind of art, but it also has startling advantages when it comes to modern informational technology. In 1990, I spoke at a UNESCO conference about the ancient Chinese concepts of "information" and "communication". Communication is a modern concept, but the Chinese had a surprisingly modern understanding of it when they invented the ancient Chinese characters. The word "通訊" (communication) in Chinese has two characters, which do not stem from hieroglyphics, but were formed according to radicals from Chinese characters. The Chinese word "辶" means to transfer, "甬" means channel, "言" means information, and "凡" means general. These four radicals together make up the two characters that comprise tongxun, which mean "broad news that can be spread through certain channels". This is the definition of " communication" in today's terms.

When I finished speaking about the amazing nature of Chinese characters, the foreign scientists, authors, engineers and officials of the U.N., along with the rest of the audience, were all taken by surprise saying, " Chinese culture is amazing!" " It seems to me that unless one understands Chinese, he cannot be considered a true intellectual." " The sky is the limit for Chinese information technology!"

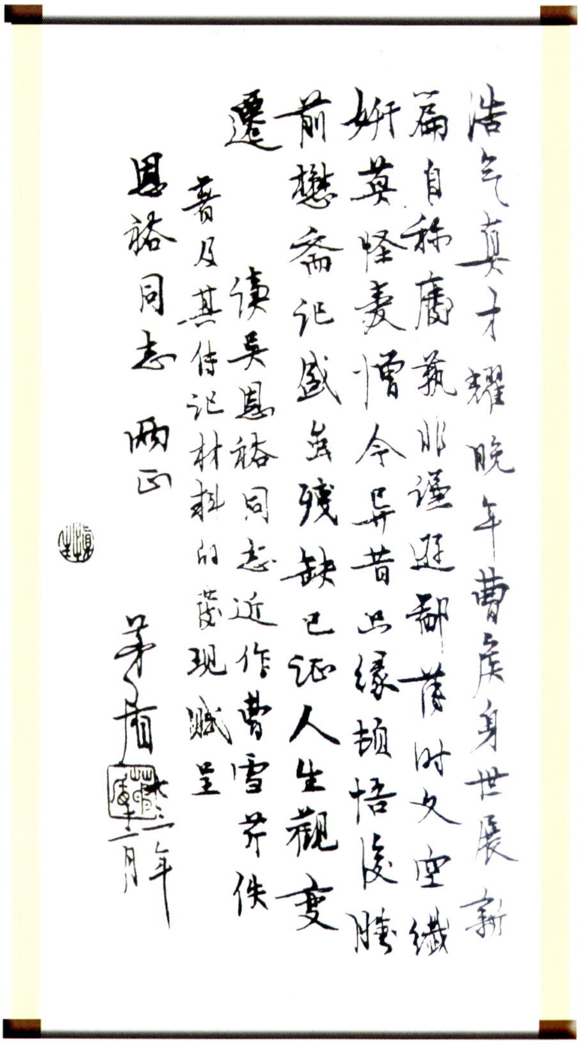

The handwriting of Maodun, one of the three most famous Chinese writers of the 20th century. As a calligrapher, he has a style of his own.

Lantingxu, by the well-known ancient Chinese calligrapher Wang Xizhi (321-379 or 303-361).

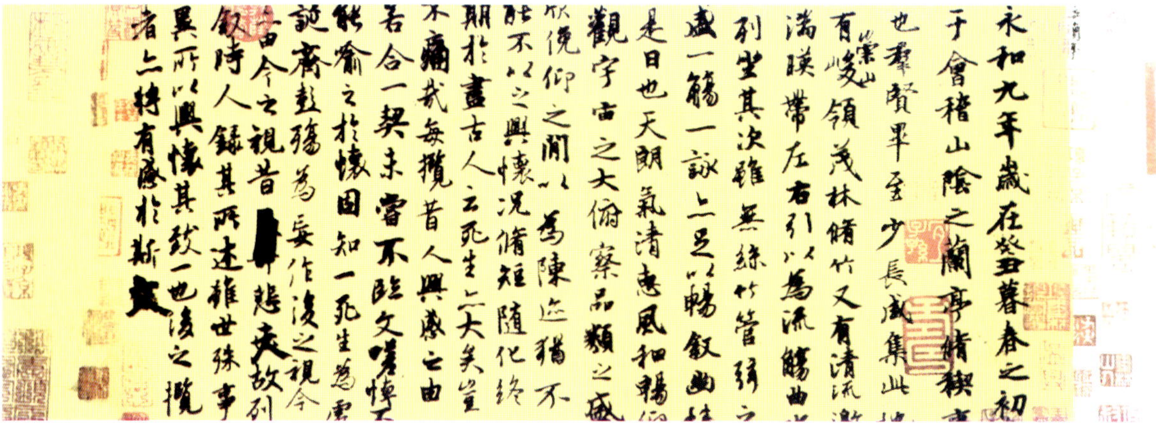

Whether you've spent one day here or six, I'd like to ask you: What have you seen? What have you thought about? I'd like to remind you that we are all from the same world. We all have the same experience of bondage and pestilence in the 18th century, of aggression and hunger in the 19th century, of war and destruction of the environment in the 20th. We also have the same dream of realizing peace and development—peace and sustainable world development now in the 21st century. Beijing is a city with a passion for this peace, a passion for this development. If you love Beijing, please feel free to make any comments. Wherever you may come from, the next time you visit Beijing, you will — as if you were in your own hometown — see your dream.

Appendix 1 Chronology of Beijing's Historical Events

- Some half a million years ago, Peking man lived in Zhoukoudian, Fangshan District in the southwestern suburbs of Beijing. The complete skull of Peking Man was discovered in 1929.
- In East Hulin Village of western Beijing's Mentougou District, a tomb containing three bodies was discovered. The bodies were dated to be ten thousand years old.
- Five thousand years ago, in Changping District's Xueshan Village, sites of early human activities were discovered in the 1960s. A great deal of pottery was also excavated.
- 3,000 years ago, the ancient site of the city of Ji was discovered in Dongjialin of Fangshan District. It was the earliest town in the region of modern-day Beijing.
- In 221 B.C., the Qin Dynasty started construction on the Great Wall, to the north of Beijing.
- 1st century. During the Han Dynasty, the city of Beijing moved to Xuanwu District-today's city center, and the city of Ji was constructed. The Han Dynasty continued to build the Great Wall to the north of Beijing to prevent attacks from the Huns. The Dabaotai Han Grave, dating to this time period, has been discovered and excavated (located in Beijing's Fengtai District). During the 8th Century, the city of Ji became the political center of northern China. At present, more than 200 pottery wells of the 8th Century have been uncovered. During this time, the Silk Road connecting Europe and Asia was opened.
- 938 A.D. The city of Ji became co-capital of the Liao Dynasty. This was the first time that Beijing became the capital. The time population is 150 thousand.
- In 1151 A.D. the Jin Dynasty (1115-1234) of northern China founded its capital at the Lotus Pool near the city of Ji. The total area of the city was 22 square kilometers, and the population was 400,000.
- 1261 A.D. Emperor Kublai Khan(1215-1294, reigned 1260-1294) of the Yuan Dynasty ordered his capital built in the north of modern-day Beijing, with Beihai as it's center. 1274 A.D. Dadu of the Yuan Dynasty was built, covering an area of 30.2 Square kilometers, with a population of 950,000.
- 1405-1433 A.D. Emperor Zhu Di (1360-1424, reigned 1402-1424)of the Ming Dynasty sent Zheng He on seven expeditions to the western seas. But from that time until the overthrow of the Qing Dynasty, there were no more large-scale voyages.
- 1406-1420 A. D. Emperor Zhu Di (1360-1424, reigned 1402-1424) of the Ming Dynasty started to build the Forbidden City.
- 1421 A.D. The Ming Dynasty officially moved its capital from Nanjing to Beijing, while Nanjing still retained its capital status in a sense.
- 1473 A.D. The Ming Dynasty restored the Great Wall.
- 1605 A.D. Matteo Ricci (1552-1610), an Italian Jesuit missionary, built the Southern Cathedral in Beijing.
- 1616 A.D. Emperor Nurhachu (1559-1626) of the Qing Dynasty founded "The State of Jin", which was called "Hou-Jin" afterwards.
- In 1644 A.D. the Qing Dynasty founded its capital in Beijing, and took the Forbidden City as its imperial palace. Emperor Shunzhi (reigned from 1644-1661) appointed the German Catholic missionary Tang Ruowang (Johann Adam Schall von Bell, 1591-1666) to the establishment of a new calendar.
- 1662 A.D. Zheng Chenggong (1624-1662) recovered Taiwan from the Dutch.
- 1688 A.D. Emperor Qing Shengzu Kangxi (reigned 1661-1722) received the French Boanerges, learning much from them about modern science and knowledge.
- 1696 A.D. Emperor Qing Shengzu Kangxi completely crushed rebellions in the regions of Xinjiang and Inner Mongolia.
- 1706 A.D. The Tibetan local authority sent a false Dalai to Beijing.
- 1717 A.D. Emperor Qing Shengzu Kangxi called into effect the law of Foreign Trade by Merchant Ships, which restricted merchant ships sailing abroad as well as foreign trade. China began to adopt the policy of isolation.
- 1744 A.D. The Italian Boanerges Giuseppe Castiglione (Lang Shining, 1688-1766) took part in the design of Dashuifa at Yuanmingyuan.
- 1820 A.D. The Gross National Product of China had led the world for the past century.
- 1840 A.D. The Opium War broke out as a result of opium being imported by the British.
- 1860 A.D. Anglo-French Allied Forces invaded Beijing, forayed and burned Yuanmingyuan; many invaluable antiques and treasures were destroyed.
- 1861-1908 A.D. Empress Dowager Cixi held court from behind a screen.
- 1875 A.D. Emperor Guangxu succeeded the throne.
- 1900 A.D. Anglo-French Allied Forces invaded Beijing, many cultural relics and historic sites being ruined as a result.
- 1912 A.D. The Qing Dynasty was overthrown and the Republic of China was founded, with Nanjing as its capital.
- 1925 A.D. After the last Emperor of the Qing Dynasy - Xuantong Puyi laid down the scepter, the Palace Museum was founded.
- 1931 A.D. Japan invaded Northeast China.
- July 7, 1937 A.D. The Lugou Bridge Incident broke out in Beijing, and was regarded as the beginning of Japan's complete invasion of China.
- 1945 A.D. The Second World War ended, Japan surrendered.
- October 1, 1949 A. D. The People's Republic of China was founded.
- 1978 A.D. Mr. Deng Xiaoping (1904-1997) headed the thrust for the reform and opening up of China.
- 1990 A.D. Beijing held the 11th Asian Games, with over 4,600 athletes from 34 countries and regions taking part in the games.
- July 13, 2001 A. D. Beijing won the bid to host the 2008 Olympic Games.
- 2005 A.D. China's Gross Domestic Product (GDP) ranked fourth in the world.
- Nov. 4-5, 2006 A.D. Beijing hosted the Forum on China-Africa Cooperation, with the participation of 42 heads of state or government from 48 countries.

Appendix 2 Routing designed for Beijing

Routing designed for 6-day tour

forenoon the Forbidden City
afternoon the Forbidden City
evening Dongyuan Theater of Changpuhe
or Chang'an Theater

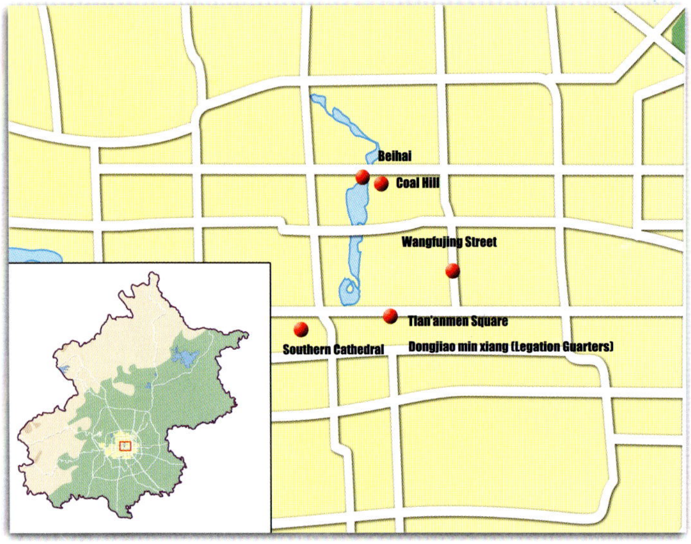

forenoon Coal Hill, Beihai, Round City
afternoon Tian'anmen Square,
Dongjiaominxiang (Legation Guarters),
Southern Cathedral
evening Wangfujing Street

forenoon Yonghegong Lamasery, Confucian temple
afternoon the Temple of Heaven,
Niujie (Ox Street) Mosque,
White Cloud Taoist Temple (Baiyunguan)
evening Quanjude Roast Duck Restaurant

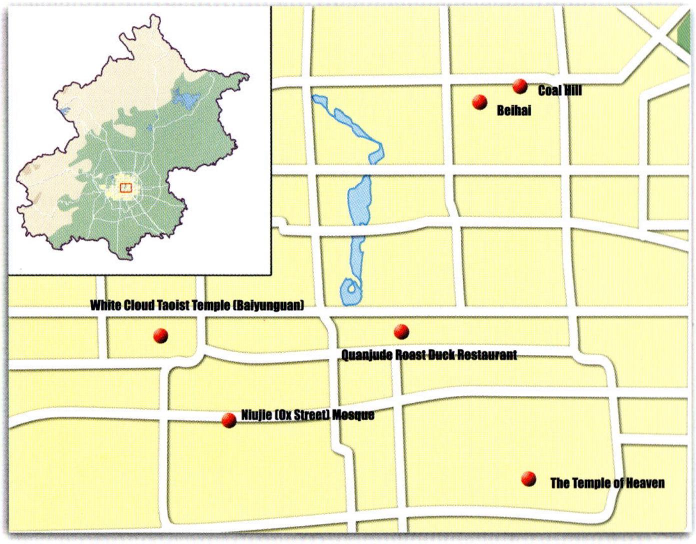

4

forenoon the Great Wall
afternoon Beijing Olympic Park
evening rest

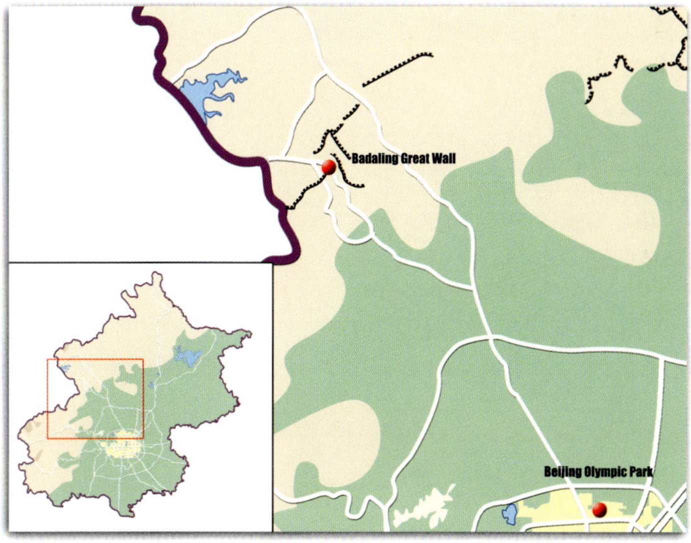

5

forenoon the Summer Palace
afternoon Fragrant Hill
evening Shicha Lake folk houses
Jiumen traditional snack town

6

forenoon the Ming Tombs
afternoon shopping in New Silk Street market and Liulichang culture street
evening rest

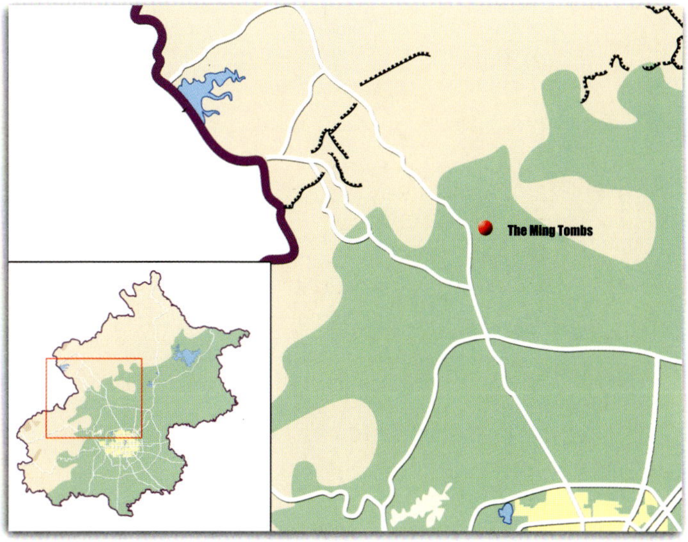

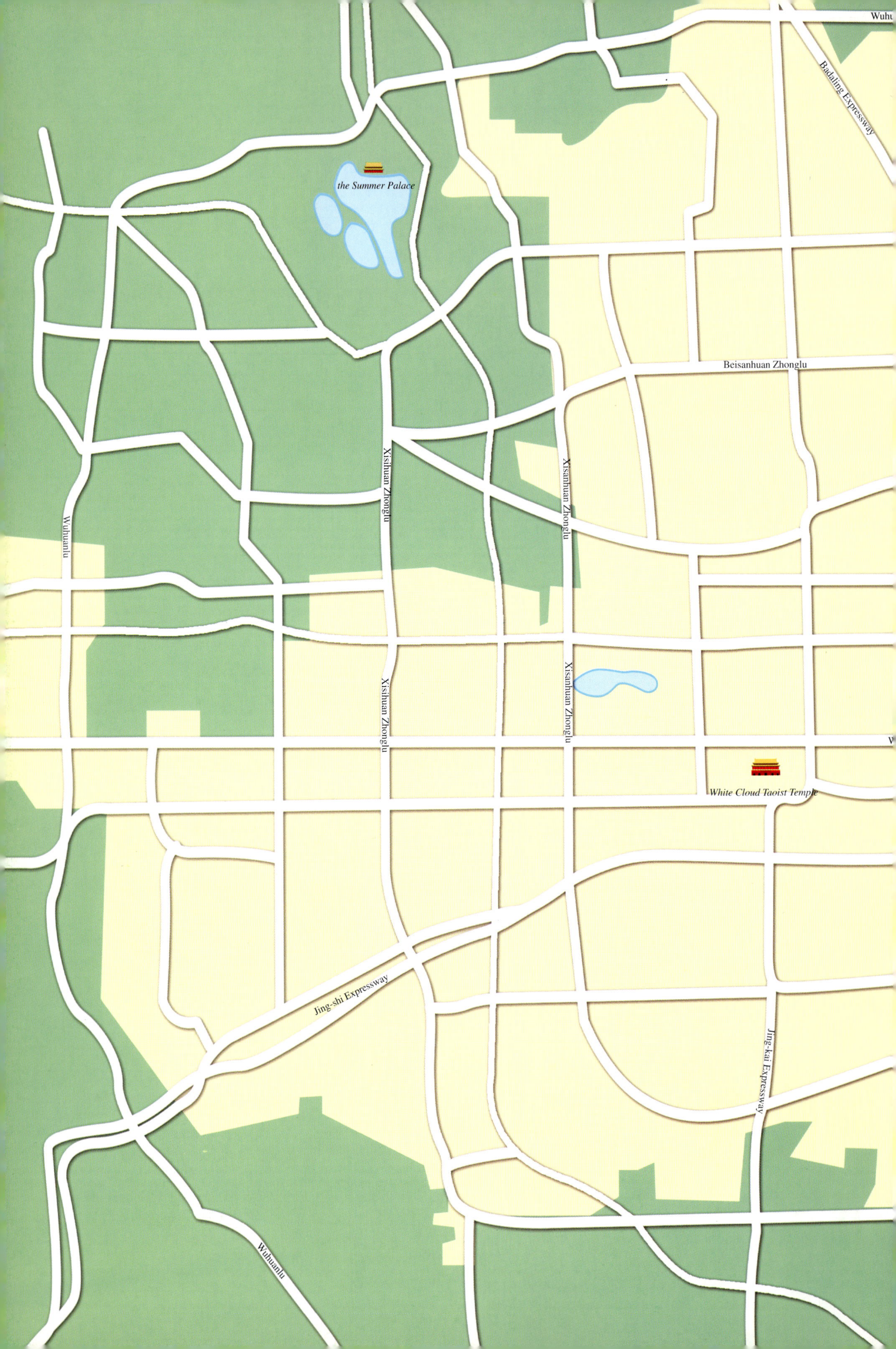

Wuhu
Badaling Expressway
the Summer Palace
Beisanhuan Zhonglu
Xisihuan Zhonglu
Xisanhuan Zhonglu
Wuhuanlu
Xisanhuan Zhonglu
Xisihuan Zhonglu
White Cloud Taoist Temple
Jing-shi Expressway
Jing-kai Expressway
Wuhuanlu

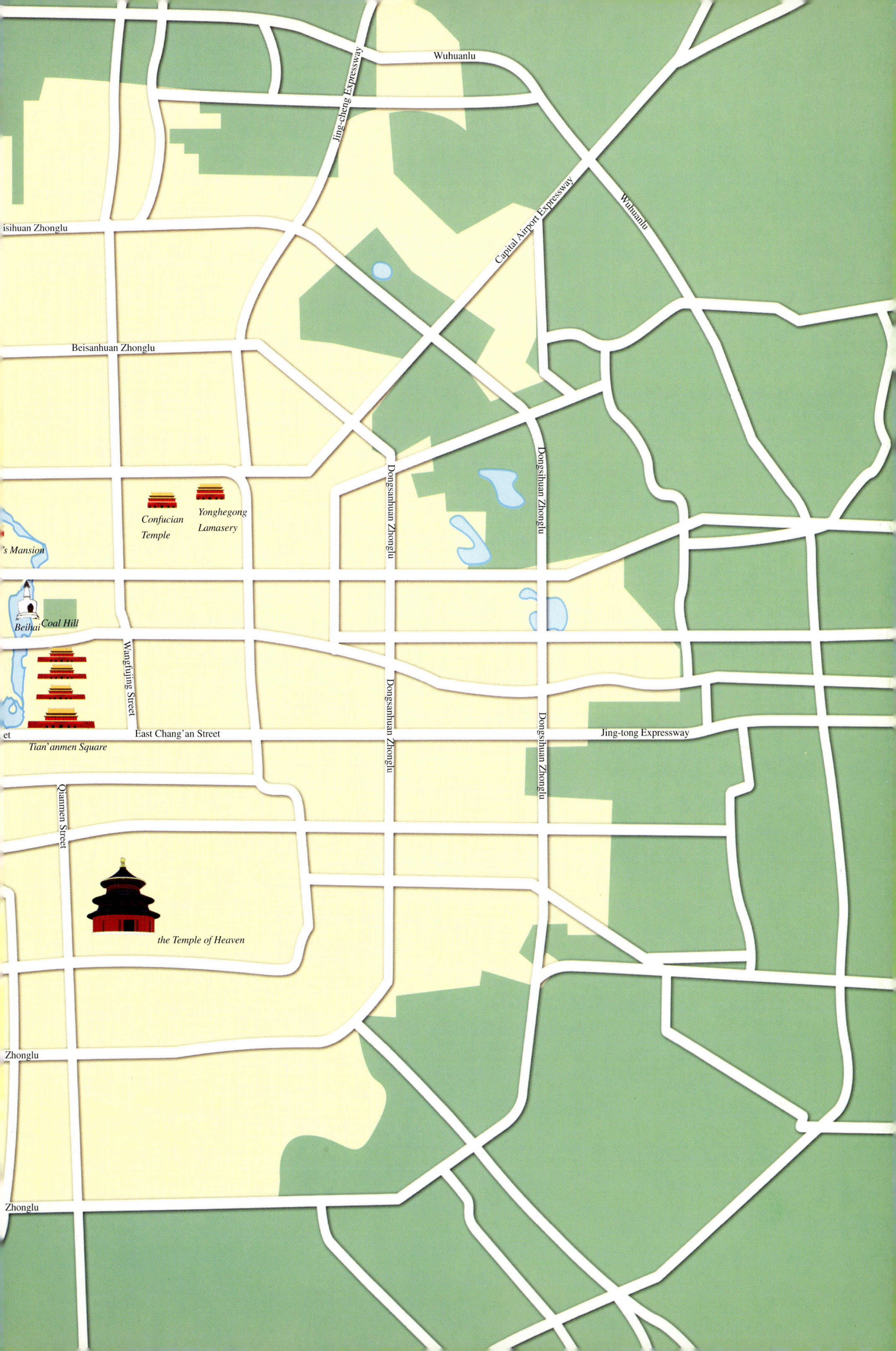

Wuhuanlu
Jing-cheng Expressway
Capital Airport Expressway
Wuhuanlu
isihuan Zhonglu
Beisanhuan Zhonglu
Dongsanhuan Zhonglu
Dongsihuan Zhonglu
Confucian Temple
Yonghegong Lamasery
's Mansion
Beihai
Coal Hill
Wangfujing Street
Dongsanhuan Zhonglu
Dongsihuan Zhonglu
et
East Chang'an Street
Jing-tong Expressway
Tian'anmen Square
Qianmen Street
the Temple of Heaven
Zhonglu
Zhonglu

Appendix 3 Beijing Routing designed for 3-day and 1-day tour

Routing designed for 3-day tour

1

forenoon the Forbidden City, Tian'anmen Square
afternoon Yonghegong Lamasery
evening Wangfujing Street

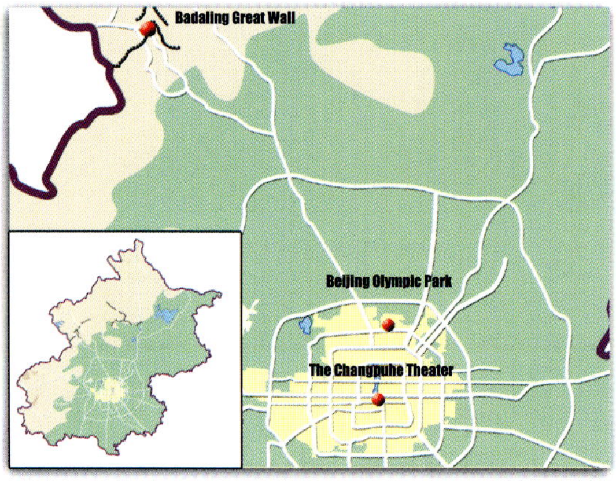

2

forenoon the Great Wall,
afternoon the Ming Tombs, Beijing Olympic Park
evening Peking Opera

3

forenoon the Summer Palace
afternoon Fragrant Hill, Yuanmingyuan
evenin Liulichang Culture Street

Routing designed for 1-day tour

forenoon

the Forbidden City,
Tian'anmen Square

afternoon

the Summer Palace

evening

Wangfujing Street

Appendix 4 telephone numbers of famous sight-seeing spots, restaurants and travel agencies

No.	Name	Tel.	note
1	Palace Museum	65132255	No. 4 Jinshan Front Street, Dongcheng District
2	Tian'anmen Square	65243322	The center of Beijing City
3	Coal Hill Park	64044071	No. 44 Jinshan West Street, Xicheng District
4	Beihai Park	64040610	No. 1 Wenjing Street, Xicheng District
5	Prince Gong's Mansion	66168149	Qianhai West Street, Xicheng District
6	The Temple of Heaven	67028866	No.7 Tiantanneidongli, Chongwen District
7	The Summer Palace	62881144	Yiheyuan Road Haidian District
8	The Ruins of Yuanmingyuan	62628501	No.28 Tsinghua West Road, Haidian District
9	Fragrant Hill Park	62591155	East of Xiaoxi Hill in Northwestern skirts of Beijing
10	Badaling Great Wall	69121308	Inside Yanqing District
11	The Ming Tombs	60761424	Tianshou Hill, Changping District
12	The Fayuan Temple	83517183	No. 7 Fayuansi Front Street, Xuanwu Street
13	Yonghegong Lamasery	64044499	No. 12 Yonghegong Street, Dongcheng District
14	White Cloud Taoist Temple	63463531	Outside Xibianmen, Xicheng District
15	Niujie (Ox Street) Mosque	63532564	No.18 Niujie, Xuanwu District
16	Xuanwu Cathedral	66037139	No.141 Qianmen West Street, Xicheng District
17	Southern Cathedral	63016678	No.129 Qianmen Street, Chongwen District
18	The Pool and Cudrania Temple	60862244	Mentougou District
19	Ordination Terrace Temple	69806611	Ma'anshan Hill, Mentougou District
20	Peking University	62752114	No.75 Haidian Road, Haidian District
21	Beichizhi Primary School	65251287	No.46 Beichizi Street, Dongcheng District
22	The Second Middle School of Beijing	65252231	No.15 Neiwubu Street, Dongcheng District
23	Tsinghua University	62785001	Haidian District
24	Beijing University of Aeronautics & Astronautics	82317114	No.37 Xueyuan Road, Haidian District
25	Quanjude Roast Duck Restaurant	65112418	No.32 Qianmen Street, Chongwen District
26	Fangshan Restaurant	64011889	Inside Beihai Park
27	Fengzeyuan Restaurant	63186688	No. 83 Zhushikou West Street, Xuanwu Districy
28	Tan cuisine	65281039	Inside Beijing Hotel, No. 33 East Chang'an Street, Dongcheng District
29	Donglaisun Restaurant (Head Office in Xindong'an Market)	65280932	Floor 5 Xindong'an Market, No. 138 Wangfujing Street, Dongcheng Distric
30	Jiumen Snack Town	64026868	Shicha Lake, Dongcheng District
31	Peace Hotel	65128833	No. 3 Jinyu Hutong, Dongcheng District
32	Beijing New Otani Chang Fu Gong Hotel	65125555	No. 26 Jianguomenwai Street, Chaoyang District
33	Brazil Grilled Meat Store	66056957	West Building of Fenghuawaijing, Caishikou, Xuanwu District
34	Moscow Restaurant	68354454	No. 135 Xiwai Street, Xicheng District
35	The Great Wall Sheraton Hotel	65905566	No. 10 Dongsanhuan North Road, Chaoyang District
36	Beijing Kempinski Hotel	64653388	No. 50 Liangmaqiao Road, Chaoyang District
37	Fragrant Hill Hotel	62591166	Inside Fragrant Hill Park, Haidian District
38	Beijing Department Store	65126677	No. 255 Wangfujing Street, Dongcheng District
39	Yansha Youyi Shopping City	64651188	No. 50 Liangmaqiao Road, Chaoyang Disreict
40	Hu-Guang Assembly Hall Theatre	63518284	No. 3 Hufang Road, Xuanwu District
41	Dongyuan Theater of Changpuhe	85115366	Inside Changpuhe Park, Dongcheng District
42	Chang'an Big Theater	65101310	No. 7 Jianguomennei Street, Dongcheng District
43	Baoli Theater	65001188	No. 14 Dongzhimen South Street, Dongcheng District
44	Tianqiao Theatre	3156337	No. 30 Beiwei Road, Xuanwu District
45	Panjiayuan Antique Market	67747711	No. 21 Dongsanhuan South Road, Chaoyang District
46	China Comfort Travel	65066923 (HQ) 0351-4605013 (Shangxi) 0314-2036977 (Chende) 021-51168163 (Shanghai) 025-86639591 (Nanjing)	No. 5 Nongzhanguan South Road, Chaoyang District
47	Beijing Tourism Group	65159420 (group) 8008101651 (holiday travel agency) 65150093 (ticket) 51296652 (overseas)	No. 28 Jianguomenwai Street
48	China Ocean International Travel	96096691 65531819 (international) 67022698 (domestic)	No. 56 Dongxinglong, Chongwen District

图书在版编目（CIP）数据

我爱北京（英文版全彩精美画册）/吴季松主编.—北京：中国发展出版社，2007.4

ISBN 978-7-80234-001-5

Ⅰ.我… Ⅱ.吴… Ⅲ.北京市－概况－画册Ⅳ.K921-64

中国版本图书馆 CIP 数据核字（2007）第 026331 号

我爱北京（英文版　全彩精美画册）

著作责任者：吴季松

出版发行：中国发展出版社

（北京市西城区百万庄大街 16 号 8 层　100037）

标准书号：ISBN 978-7-80234-001-5/K·13

经销者：各地新华书店

印刷者：人民美術印刷厂

开本：880 × 1230mm　1/16

印张：8

字数：30 千字

版次：2007 年 4 月第 1 版

印次：2007 年 4 月第 1 次印刷

印数：1—5000 册

定价：68.00 元

咨询电话：（010）68990642　68990692

购书热线：（010）68990682　68990686

网址：http://www.develpress.com.cn

电子邮件：fazhan@drc.gov.cn